Contents

KU-637-399

361.06

(HHC)

Problems in Practice

This series is the natural successor to the popular *Psychology in Action* series, and continues and extends the aim of 'giving psychology away', that is, making psychological expertise more freely available.

Each title focuses on a common problem across a number of different professions – industry, education, medicine, the police and other public and social services. The approach is practical, drawing on examples from a range of work situations. And the reader is constantly invited to look at the problem both as object and subject: accepting help as well as offering help; dealing with one's own aggressive impulses as well as those directed towards you by others; both giving and requesting expert advice. Psychologists have a great deal to say about how to improve our working lives and the aim here is to offer both practical skills and new insights.

THE AUTHORS AND EDITORS
Glynis Breakwell (Reader in Psychology, University of Surrey, Guildford)
David Fontana (Reader in Educational Psychology, University of Wales College of Cardiff)
Glenys Parry (Regional Tutor in Clinical Psychology, Knowle Hospital, Fareham and Top Grade Clinical Psychologist, Department of Psychotherapy, Royal South Hants Hospital, Southampton)

The original, problem-solving approach of this series was applied also to the creation of these titles, by a team of three, acting as both authors and editors. Each member of the team, drawing on their own practical experience, contributed ideas, material and criticism to every title, in addition to taking full responsibility for the writing of at least one of them. This approach ensures a book of wide practical relevance, combining the strengths and expertise of all authors, a uniformity of approach with a minimum of overlap between titles, yet retaining the clear, simple line of the single-authored book. The commitment of the authors to the series made all of this possible.

OTHER TITLES IN THE SERIES
Managing Stress by David Fontana
Facing Physical Violence by Glynis Breakwell
Interviewing by Glynis Breakwell
Social Skills at Work by David Fontana

Problems in Practice

COPING WITH CRISES

Glenys Parry

Regional Tutor in Clinical Psychology
Knowle Hospital, Fareham, and
Top Grade Clinical Psychologist,
Royal South Hants Hospital, Southampton

Published by The British Psychological Society
and Routledge Ltd.

For Maggie

First published in 1990 by The British Psychological Society, St Andrews House, 48 Princess Road East, Leicester, LE1 7DR, in association with Routledge Ltd, 11 New Fetter Lane, London EC4P 4EE, and in the USA by Routledge, Chapman & Hall Inc., 29 West 35th Street, New York NY 10001.

Reprinted 1992, 1993

British Library Cataloguing in Publication Data
Parry, Glenys
    Coping with crises. – (Problems in practice series)
    1. Counselling. Crisis intervention
    I. Title   II. Series
    361.3'23

    ISBN 0–901715–82–4

Library of Congress Cataloging-in-Publication Data is available

Printed in Great Britain by BPC Wheatons Ltd, Exeter

Foreword

None of us goes through life without experiencing crises. Mercifully, most of the time we're faced with nothing worse than missing our train or trying to do a dozen things when we've only time to do one, or forgetting to post a birthday card, or having to patch up a quarrel with a friend. But from time to time we face major events that threaten to take from us the things through which we orientate ourselves and find our sense of identity.

So what do we do; how do we cope? And in professional life what do we do to help others cope? How do we help them handle the distress and the bewilderment that come from being brought face to face with tragedy, whether it be the tragedy of bereavement, of sickness, of redundancy, or of any one of the devastating events that form part of the human condition?

In this sane and sensitive book, Glenys Parry addresses these issues. From her own wide experience as a clinical psychologist she looks at the nature of crises, their impact upon people, and at ways of understanding and helping those facing crises to survive and find continuing meaning and purpose in life. While never minimising the impact that a major crisis has upon the thoughts, feelings and behaviour of the individual, Dr Parry shows that even the worst crisis can be overcome through the power of the human spirit and with the guidance and support of others.

At no point does the author suggest this guidance and support should take the form of over-protecting people and attempting to insulate them from their pain and their suffering. As she makes clear, the arrival of a crisis confronts in everyone the belief that they are living in a safe world, where things like that can never happen to them. So this is not a book about encouraging people to escape from reality but, on the contrary, a book about helping them understand what reality is, and about providing them with a caring network which enables them to live within this reality. At the same time, it shows us that through helping others towards this understanding we also help ourselves. Each man or woman with whom we work is a mirror in which we see part of ourselves, and through which we can come to realise more deeply our own humanity and the way in which this humanity is common to us all.

This is a deeply felt book. And so it should be. There is no point in writing about crises unless you write from your own compassion. To read it is to feel touched as well as informed. No-one who wants to help others through difficult times can afford to ignore the insights provided in the pages that follow.

David Fontana and Glynis Breakwell
Series Editors

Chapter One

What Is A Crisis?

Crisis – the very word brings echoes of urgency, of threat and of the need for action. The word *crisis* really means a point or a time for deciding something: the turning-point, the decisive moment. Other layers of meaning have accumulated. We use the word when we are faced with an urgent, stressful situation which feels overwhelming. Crises happen to individuals, families, organisations and nations. I shall write about individuals but shall discuss them in terms of the social groups to which they belong.

This book is written for those who are called upon to help people during a crisis as part of their everyday work. There are few professional workers and managers who do not come into contact with people in crisis, whether a nurse caring for the victim of a road accident, a teacher trying to reach an unhappy student, a police officer intervening in a street fight or a doctor breaking bad news. Social workers have frequent contact with crisis and are sometimes trained in crisis work. Often, like other professionals, they are expected to 'pick it up as they go along', without any special preparation. Others who work with crises include health visitors, midwives, probation officers, educational welfare officers, the clergy, personnel managers and those working for voluntary care agencies. Although it is not primarily aimed at specialists, some psychologists, psychotherapists or crisis counsellors may find the book interesting. Nor is it a self-help book, but I hope it would be useful to someone wrestling with a crisis.

Perhaps this book is rather unusual in the way it sets out to help you help others. It has been my experience that the best crisis workers do not follow a rigid set of rules when helping others. It seems to me that there are three qualities which distinguish the effective helpers:

▶ they have an internal 'map' of the psychology of crisis;

▶ they understand how professional help can complement the person's own resources;

▶ and they have a deep empathy with the person's predicament.

This book aims to help you develop these qualities in yourself rather than giving you specific advice about what to do in a crisis, although I have tried to include plenty of practical information too. Because this approach is unusual it might be helpful to explain it in more detail.

Helping someone in a crisis is like a journey. You will inevitably be faced with unknown territory. However experienced you are, each time you help someone through a crisis you will find you are travelling a new path. There are very many different routes to a constructive resolution of the crisis. Equally, there are numerous ways of getting lost. What you need is a map which will help you orientate yourself so that you help the person move in the right direction. In order to act as a guide on this journey, you need a general understanding of the psychology of crisis, knowledge of the 'natural history' of crisis, from onset to resolution. You need to understand the psychology of coping and of how people seek and receive help. You need a means of recognising where the person is on the journey towards resolving the crisis, because the one you are trying to help will not have an objective view. When you have this mental map, you can safely use your discretion about what to do in a specific situation. You will be able to choose how best to intervene and can also pass your knowledge on, either to the crisis victim or to others who are trying to help.

Professional help should go hand-in-hand with the person's own resources. The skilled helper is not necessarily the one who 'takes over' and organises everything. There may be times when the crisis victim does require that level of dependency, but these are very rare. The priority is to help others to help themselves, and there are many good reasons for this. The professional worker is a very small part of the person's social milieu, has only a limited amount of time available and should not usurp the role of a parent, a spouse or even a friend. It is very easy for professional help to 'disable' people by making them feel childlike and helpless rather than 'enable' them to use their own internal resources and the resources of their social environment. The nurse, the doctor, the police officer, the social worker, the teacher, the manager have this in common in relation to the people they work with, whether patients, clients, students, employees or the general public. Each can act as a catalyst, enhancing the person's use of his or her own resources.

Each can be a positive force to facilitate constructive coping during a crisis and so increase the individual's self-respect.

Finally, a mental map and a desire that people should be treated as resourceful adults are not enough by themselves. Without empathy, they could even be damaging. Empathy is not the same as sympathy; indeed, feeling sorry for people is not in itself a good basis for helping them. Empathy is a capacity to feel something of what the other person is feeling, to look at the world through their eyes. What is the best way to achieve a deeper empathy with the people you are hoping to help? The basis of empathy is a form of identification with the other person. This identification stems from a common humanity, an awareness (in the words of the Roman writer Terence) that 'nothing human is alien to me'. Empathic 'knowing' is different from objective, detached 'knowing about'. You can know a lot *about* a person with *knowing* them at all. You can know a great deal about 'crisis intervention' or 'crisis theory' without knowing crisis from the inside. The only way to develop empathy is to go beyond the labels 'professional' and 'client' in one's own mind and to understand the human suffering within oneself. For this reason, much of this book is written to help you understand your own crises as much as other people's. It does not draw a false distinction between 'them' (the people in crisis we try to help) and 'us' (we professionals who are above such a messy and painful business). I have tried to bring the theoretical 'map' to life by asking you to relate it to your own life and to make sense of your own suffering. Many of the self-assessment exercises are designed to lead you into a deeper empathic grasp of the issues. When this *empathy* is combined with the *objectivity* of the internal map and the genuine desire to *foster independence*, one creates a powerful force for good.

In summary, this is a book for anyone who works with people suffering crisis or its aftermath. It can equally well be read by their clients, because it aims to give readers a basic understanding of crisis and to relate this to their own experience. It is difficult to learn a set of 'rules' from a book about how to respond to someone in crisis; better to discover some basic principles about the process which will change the way you think about it and thus the way you respond. It is not very valuable to learn about crisis in the abstract; better to think through these issues in relation to realistic examples and, best of all, one's own life. This is not another handbook on crisis intervention, but a way to explore what you know about crisis, to deepen your understanding as well as helping you learn practical ways of being an effective helper.

Although we can prevent many crises, sometimes they overtake us whatever we do. Despite this, there is a great deal we can do to ensure that we are not damaged by them, and indeed that we gain as much as possible from the experience. It is easy to say 'every crisis is an opportunity in disguise' (some people even point out that the Chinese pictogram for crisis combines 'danger' with 'opportunity'), but this is cold comfort to someone in the throes of one. Anyone who has faced a severely stressful life event knows the pain and misery it causes. I believe it is only by facing and tolerating the pain that the hidden opportunity for personal development is revealed. Tolerating pain is easier if the reason for that pain is understood.

Everyone reading this book will fall into one of three categories: those who have had a major life crisis, those who are currently facing one, and those who are going to have one. It is a fiction that we can avoid crisis altogether – birth and death are universal human crises, and in between there are many opportunities for life to confront us with the unmanageable. Although we cling to this fiction for comfort and security, it leaves us very vulnerable when crisis strikes. One of the things which makes it so difficult to cope constructively is the underlying belief 'This shouldn't be happening to me'. The disillusioning part of crisis – the realisation that we are not living in a safe, just world but one where horrible things happen arbitrarily to people – is hard to bear.

This book will examine what is and is not a crisis, using a range of examples. It will show what makes crises so stressful and how they can be damaging to health and well-being, not just at the time but for years afterwards. Yet good can come from them and people can benefit in the long run. A crisis presents a challenge to our development, and if this is accepted it is a spur to growth and new learning.

Everyone has their own common-sense understanding of crisis, and this forms the basis of the 'internal map'. Before reading any further, you should complete Exercise 1. This will give you a starting-point to explore your current views about crisis and a way to check later how these have developed through reading the book.

FORMS OF LOSS

Some kinds of crisis hit the headlines – such as major disasters, aeroplane crashes and murders. Although these events are undoubtedly especially traumatic (and I shall discuss them later), in fact they are not very common compared to 'everyday' crises – bereavement, marital break-down, illness, job loss. Let's begin by examining some of these common-or-garden events to outline the anatomy of crisis, starting with bereavement.

ATTITUDES TO CRISIS QUIZ

EXERCISE 1

Read each item and give it a score from 1 to 5 on the following scale:

1 = Definitely no, I disagree strongly.

2 = No, I disagree.

3 = I don't feel strongly one way or the other.

4 = Yes, I agree.

5 = Yes, definitely. I agree strongly.

When you have completed the quiz, keep your scores in a safe place – you will be invited to repeat the questions after you have read this book and explore how your attitudes to crisis have changed!

1. It is always better to avoid a crisis if you can. ☐

2. People usually make their own crises. ☐

3. Crises just happen, often there is nothing you can do to prevent them. ☐

4. It takes about three months to recover from a bereavement. ☐

5. It is best to try and take your mind off things if you are feeling very upset. ☐

6. There is always something to be learned from a crisis. ☐

7. Once a person is very anxious or depressed, there is not much they can do about it themselves. ☐

8. If someone is experiencing horrifying 'flashbacks' to a crisis event it means they are suffering from a post traumatic stress disorder. ☐

9. Professional health workers generally know how to handle a crisis. ☐

10. You are more likely to have an accident following a stressful event. ☐

11. Professional help is usually needed if someone has had a severely stressful event. ☐

12. After most crises it is best to get things back to normal as quickly as possible. ☐

13. It's just a matter of luck if you get the right kind of help during a crisis. ☐

14. Crisis is what happens when your emotions get out of control. ☐

Answers to Exercise 1 can be found at the end of the book on page 112.

❏ *It was just an ordinary day for Meg Brown. She was making a cup of coffee for herself and her husband Jack, and wondering whether to visit her sister later on. She could hear Jack in the shower and suddenly heard him shout that there weren't any towels. She shouted back 'You should have thought of that sooner', but after a while she relented and went to the airing cupboard. When she tried to open the bathroom door, something was blocking it. Through the crack she glimpsed Jack sitting on the floor pressed up against the door. He didn't move and didn't speak to her when she asked him what was the matter. She couldn't open the door to help him and couldn't see what was going on. Frightened, she ran next door for help. Her neighbour came and climbed in through the bathroom window while Meg called an ambulance. But Jack was dead.*

It sounds dramatic, but this type of event is quite common. Over 60,000 men like Jack die of acute cardiac failure in Britain every year. Bereavement is the most striking form of *loss*, although, as we shall see later, many crises have an element of loss: for example, divorce, disability or the birth of a handicapped child. For Meg a nightmare has begun. Her everyday world has been shattered, but she doesn't – she can't – realise that immediately. It is not just that she is faced with loneliness and many new demands. All her plans, shared goals which involved her husband, will have to be abandoned or modified. Her husband provided her with many things, some of which she has ceased even to notice but will now become aware of. Most of all, she knew who she was because of her relationship to him, and not just in a straightforward way ('I am Jack's wife'): through countless repetitive interactions, day after day, she saw herself reflected in the mirror of his relationship to her. Almost all her friends, neighbours and relatives knew Meg as part of a couple rather than an individual, and she realises that no one knows her the way he knew her. The crisis is not just that she has lost Jack. She has lost herself.

So it is with all losses – we don't know who we are any more. We have to go on living to find that out, but it is frightening. And it hurts. People underestimate the sheer physical pain of grief. I shall return to that later.

Meg's bereavement illustrates another feature of crisis: the events producing it are outside her control. This is particularly true of bereavement, less true of other crises. But whether or not the individual could have influenced events, it always *feels uncontrollable*; this is one of the central features of the victim's experience of crisis.

Next, consider a very different form of marital loss:

❏ *Janice and Pete Bowers had been married six years and had two daughters, aged five and three. Pete, a self-employed decorator, often worked all hours, but Janice understood they needed the money – although she would have liked to see*

more of him. Recently, when he came home he had seemed tired and irritable.
More than once he had been drinking. They never seemed to talk to each other
about anything any more, just the practicalities of the home, the children, the
shopping and so on. Janice didn't get out much. She had lost touch with most of
her own friends from before she was married, and apart from her mum and dad,
who lived nearby, she didn't see many people. She wasn't really complaining,
though. She liked the way Pete had done up their home, and felt that despite their
problems they were basically a happy couple. When the girls were older and money
was less tight, they'd have more time together.

It happened one Saturday night. After quite a bit of persuasion, Pete had said
he'd be back early and take Janice and the girls to the seaside. Four o'clock, five
o'clock, six o'clock came round and still no Pete. Eventually Janice put the girls to
bed and phoned up her mum, feeling angry and disappointed but also worried.
Her mother told her that a friend of hers had seen Peter in a car with a woman. She
advised Janice to 'have it out with him'. Pete didn't come home until gone ten
o'clock. He was sullen and looked at her as if she were a stranger. They had a big
row. At first, Pete denied seeing another woman, but eventually he told her he had
been having an affair. It had been going on for two years. He said that marrying
Janice had been a mistake – he felt he had been pushed into it by Janice's parents.
He said he hadn't wanted her to find out, he thought it was best if she didn't, but
now he was glad it had all come out into the open.

Like Meg, Janice has experienced a loss – the loss of the marriage she
thought she had. Like Meg's, all her plans which concern herself in terms
of her husband have to be drastically changed. We are constantly, without always being aware of it, orientating ourselves to the future. We
don't often consciously sit down and think through our goals – we tend
to take them for granted – but nevertheless they are there. Janice had an
imagined future which consisted of thoughts and images about having a
nice home, and Pete not having to work so hard because they would
have more money. She attributed many of their difficulties to finance,
and did not doubt her husband's fundamental commitment to her and
to the children. In this sense she was wrong, she made a mistake. On the
other hand, Pete, for his own reasons, continued to give her plenty of
evidence that she was right; he went along with her view of their marriage whilst developing another set of goals of his own. The crisis comes
when he reveals his hidden self. Characteristically, this is not done sensitively and carefully but 'just happens', in a confused, painful and emotionally charged encounter. As a result, Janice has undergone a *negative*
revelation – a common feature of crisis and an extremely distressing one.

There is something uniquely painful about suddenly discovering that
something which affects you profoundly has been going on for some
time behind your back. It undermines one's understanding of reality. In

Janice's case, it also produces a powerful *humiliation*. This is a blow to one's image of oneself which causes a burning, hurtful shame. It is surprising how often this is a feature of crisis, and how frequently it is the most distressing part of all. The next vignette illustrates this:

◻ *Gerald White had a good job as head teacher of the local comprehensive school, and he and his wife Jennifer were active in a number of community groups – Gerald, for example, was treasurer of the local amateur dramatic society. He felt reasonably satisfied with his life. He never seemed to get enough time in the house to do the odd jobs that accumulated, but when the summer holidays came round he decided to make a determined effort. He and his wife went into town on the first day of the holiday, deciding to shop separately and meet each other for a drink later.*

Gerald went to a large hardware store and purchased several items, including tins of paint, paintbrushes, a small stepladder and some other bits and pieces. He paid by cheque, but inadvertently did not pay for the ladder. He had propped it up near the door without realising that the cashier hadn't seen it. He was putting the ladder in the boot of his car when he was approached by a woman who asked him if he had just purchased it. When he said he had, she told him she was a store detective and that she had reason to believe that he had not paid for the ladder.

Despite Gerald's bewildered protestations of innocence, the police were called, and to his horror he found that he was the object of a routine prosecution. He was taken to meet Jennifer, who was upset to see her husband arrive in a police car – especially as she was sitting with some friends. After he had been charged, Gerald and Jennifer discussed what to do. After all, whatever the result of the court case, it would get into the papers, and all their friends would know – 'Head teacher accused of shoplifting!'. Even though he knew he wasn't guilty, Gerald had never felt so ashamed and humiliated. He could hardly bear to look Jennifer in the face.

Here the crisis involves some material threat to Gerald, in that there is a chance that his career will be damaged by the event, leading to loss of power or income. However, by far the greater threat is to Gerald's self-image. This also illustrates how the same event might or might not be a crisis, depending on the individual and the circumstances. If Gerald did not hold a 'respectable' position within the local community, if he and his family or friends were used to brushes with the police or if he believed that getting away with nicking the odd item was fair and reasonable, the whole episode would carry far less significance. In this sense, it is Gerald's own values and social circumstances which produce the crisis.

Comparing Gerald's predicament with Janice's, we discover another dimension of crisis – *unexpectedness*. Janice's crisis has its roots in the past, whereas Gerald's and Meg's arrive entirely out of the blue. In fact, most crises are more like Janice's in this respect. They build up gradually and, looking back, it is possible to see that there have been warning signs that all is not well. However, often it is possible to see this only with the benefit of hindsight. Most crises *feel* unexpected to the people experiencing them. Take this example:

> ❑ *George Dee was proud of his record of service to his firm. He had joined as a young man and worked his way up to quite a senior position, with responsibility for a £3m. budget. His marriage had not been very happy, but George coped. He gave more and more of his time to the firm, travelling all over the country on business. He was well rewarded. Although he and his wife were growing apart and he did not see much of his children, he knew he was valued and needed. He had the respect of his seniors, a good salary, and he didn't mind in the least working long hours.*
>
> *Things started going wrong when he was passed over for promotion. He couldn't believe it when he heard that a younger person had been appointed, and someone who had joined the firm only two years previously. He made his views about it known pretty widely within the firm. He started to hint that he might be looking for something else if he didn't get the promotion he knew he deserved. A year later the company had a new managing director, someone he didn't like. Soon after this, a very difficult situation arose in his section, where his budget was exceeded – the savings targets had been totally unrealistic, and George knew he wasn't the only manager with this problem. However, they seemed to blow it up out of all proportion. He began to feel someone had it in for him; his colleagues sensed this and steered clear of him. There seemed to be no one he could talk to. He hadn't talked to his wife about anything important for a number of years. Apart from anything else, George didn't like to admit he was having trouble – he always gave a confident, coping impression to people. When the blow came, it wasn't entirely unexpected, but George still couldn't believe it. 'We're letting you go, George; it's the best thing on both sides'. After thirty years – to be pushed out of his job.*

George had been having problems for years but didn't know it. With hindsight, he will come to realise that he had been unwise to invest all his energy and time in his work at the expense of loving attachments – with his wife, for example. Without realising it, he was defining himself totally in terms of this one firm's valuation of him – very tempting in the years when it gave him easy opportunities for success and security. The marriage, on the other hand, was not so easy, and would have required hard work and perhaps facing some painful emotions. There were also ways in which George could not adjust to the changing organisational climate. He knew only one set of rules and, even when he had messages that things were changing, found it difficult to change his own attitudes and behaviour. When the crisis arose, he was unprepared. All his views about himself as a strong, competent businessman were challenged, and he was stripped of the resources he used to feel good about himself.

The features of uncontrollability, loss and humiliation are present here, with two other aspects of crisis – *uncertainty* and *change in routine*. George does not know what the future holds now. Will he be able to get another job or not? How will his wife react? Will people pity him or judge him? How will his standard of living be affected? He just doesn't have the answers to these questions. He has moved from a predictable world into an unpredictable one, and his daily habits and routines are disrupted. It is as if he doesn't know the rules for daily life in the new situation. George's mental processes are geared up for certain tasks and events – taking decisions, completing reports, organising other people's time – and now these will cease to be part of his day. This in itself is stressful and disorientating.

DANGER AND TRAUMA

So far we have seen how a crisis can be unexpected and uncontrollable, can concern loss, negative revelation and humiliation, and bring new levels of uncertainty and disruption of daily routine. None of the crises we have examined places the victim in direct physical danger; even so, each one threatens the individual's image of the self and personal plans for the future. Some crises do contain an element of danger, with a threat to life itself.

☐ *Helen Smith was soaping herself in the bath last thing at night when she discovered a small, hard lump in her right breast. She hadn't been consciously examining herself; she just felt it by accident. Immediately she felt herself go cold and there was a horrible sinking feeling inside. She carried on with her bath and told herself that it would probably turn out to be nothing. As Helen was divorced and lived with her two teenage children, she didn't have anyone she could confide in straight away. For a few hours she kept returning to feel the lump, convincing herself it was real and not her imagination. She slept badly.*

Next morning she went to the doctor, hoping to hear a quick reassurance. Instead the doctor made an appointment for her to go into hospital for a biopsy operation. It surprised her how quickly she was due to go in – there seemed hardly any time to think about it. She confided in her closest friend, who helped her with the practicalities of looking after the children. After the operation, a hospital doctor came to see her. Helen kept thinking how very young he was and wondering why he didn't look at her whilst he told her that the lump had been removed and that, yes, it was malignant. He started to tell her about what would happen next, but she couldn't take it in. He asked her if she had any questions, but she couldn't think of anything to ask. Soon she found herself alone. Everyone carried on as if nothing had happened, but the phrase 'this is it, then' kept going round in her head.

Helen, like most people, has heard or read the word *cancer* hundreds of times, always associating it with painful lingering illness and death. She has no first-hand experience of cancer at all, so she is faced with an enormous unknown. This brings an equally enormous fear – in fact she is terrified. The element of *danger* is present, but in the absence of any realistic information about her chances of survival. Even if she did know what her chances were, this event would still be a crisis for her, since it brings her face to face with *knowledge of her own mortality.*

Most of us, especially if we are young, find the idea of our own death, of the world continuing to exist without us, literally unthinkable. We know as an abstract fact that it is going to happen but we do not accept it. We avoid the reality of it in everyday life whenever possible, helped to do so by a society in which the sight of everyday, prosaic death is hidden as if it were obscene. At the same time, we have an unreal contact with violent death, through daily reports in the media and fictional accounts in novels, films and plays. These thousands of filmed or enacted deaths do nothing to bring the ordinary reality of our own end closer to us – on the contrary, they make death something 'out there' that happens to other people. This is why, for most people, any event that forces us up against the truth of our own mortality is going to be a crisis, even if we are not in danger.

For some people, unlike Helen, there is very little uncertainty about the outcome, as the diagnosis itself is news of one's own forthcoming death.

❏ *Paul Stanton had known he was gay since his early teens. It wasn't easy coming to terms with it, and the only people he'd tried to confide in (his vicar and the doctor) had given him unhelpful advice, suggesting that it was just a phase he was going through and that he should try to meet a nice girl. He didn't want that kind of advice. He wanted someone to understand him, but he felt he couldn't tell his parents. He wanted to meet a young man and have a relationship. He wanted to know what that kind of sex was like. When he was sixteen he found out – and liked it. He left home a year later and went to live in London. He did a few different jobs, but most of his energies went into the 'gay scene' – there was no shortage of partners for an attractive young man out for a good time. After a while, though, he grew tired of the same routine. Casual sex was losing its allure. He decided to study for some more qualifications, to find a more interesting job, perhaps buy his own place. About this time he met Toby. This relationship was different: he had more fun and felt more real with Toby than with anyone. They had their ups and downs, but after four years they seemed to have made a successful relationship.*

They, like almost everyone else they knew, were dismayed and frightened by the news from the States about Acquired Immune Deficiency Syndrome – AIDS. Before long it was more than just a scary rumour. They knew people who knew someone who had it. Soon one of their own friends was admitted to hospital and, despite treatment, continued to have relapses and to become weaker and more cadaverous every time they saw him. After their friend's death they joined a volunteer group to befriend AIDS victims. Paul was undecided about whether to take a test to see if he was carrying the virus; but after talking it over, he and Toby agreed that there wasn't any point in him doing so.

In the event, Paul didn't have to wait long. It started with a cold that just wouldn't clear up. He began to feel totally exhausted and started to lose weight. Now he did go for tests and treatment. On the day he went to the clinic for the results of his tests, he said to Toby that he already knew the diagnosis. It was still a shock when the doctor told him. It was one week before his twenty-fifth birthday.

Paul was well-informed enough to know what the AIDS diagnosis meant: in the current state of medical knowledge, his chances of survival were slim. Although he could not be sure exactly how long he had left, he knew that, unless there was a breakthrough, he had to come to terms with losing his life. This revelation, like no other, can drain life of its meaning, especially when the news is so untimely. Paul has the added difficulty that his illness is socially feared and the subject of widespread misunderstanding, many people believing, for example, that it can be transmitted by sharing cutlery or simply by touching. He is also faced with telling his parents, from whom he has concealed his sexual orientation and lifestyle.

Not all terminal illnesses have these complications, but very few are straightforward. All demand from the dying person that they face a time-limited future. This means one can no longer hold on to the comfortable fantasy of unlimited time in which to achieve unnamed things, in which to sort out problems or to be rewarded for past sacrifice. Quite apart from this massive psychological burden for the victim, any such crisis places strain on the relationships which sustain them through the process of coming to terms with death.

All the crises discussed so far are acutely stressful. Sometimes events happen which are so unexpected, violent and dangerous that they can be termed *traumatic*. The distinction between traumatic and non-traumatic stress is not a clear one, but trauma has the quality of a sudden, massive and overwhelming threat to the individual's safety. Traumatic stress is characteristic of disasters: recent British examples would be the Bradford football stadium fire, the Zeebrugge ferry capsizing, the King's Cross tube fire, the Hungerford massacre, the Clapham train crash, the Lockerbie and M1 air disasters and the Hillsborough football crowd tragedy. The horror of such events lies in the number of people caught up in them. Whole communities are involved, and often families suffer multiple bereavements. The staff trying to help the victims are themselves faced with traumatic emotions. This psychic pain has an unbearable quality.

It is easy to forget that traumatic stress happens to people every day. If you were to add up the number of victims in all the disasters mentioned above, it would not equal the deaths in Britain alone from road traffic accidents in an average two month period.

Driving back on the motorway from a lovely day visiting gardens and garden centres, Jill Black and her close friend Peggy were in good spirits. They had been discussing the gardens they had seen and debating the virtues of a flower border devoted to one colour group. It had developed into a kind of game – how many grey and white plants they could think of. Jill was driving well within the motorway speed limit as she always did, but suddenly in front of them a car went out of control, spun round and bounced off the central barrier. In a reflex action, Jill wrenched the steering wheel to the left to avoid hitting the car. In a squeal of brakes, other cars also started to swerve and skid. Jill and Peggy were thrown violently around as their car, now out of control, slewed round, skidded backwards, collided with an oncoming car, hit the bank near the hard shoulder and turned over completely, coming to rest at a steep angle on the bank.

Jill was dazed, but found she was able to move. She got out of the car as quickly as possible and tried to help Peggy. Peggy was not moving. Her head was bleeding and her side of the car was crumpled in like an old tin can. Her legs seemed trapped. The scene in front of Jill was horrifying: about a dozen cars were piled up; some were sickeningly smashed in. People were shouting and screaming. A child was crying. Drivers further down had pulled up and put on their hazard lights. Jill was tugging and tugging at Peggy's door but could not move it. Her only thought was to get Peggy out because the car might catch fire. It seemed to Jill as if she were completely unreal – as if this were a film she was watching or a nightmare she was dreaming. She tried to run to find someone to help her, but her legs gave way and she fell over. It was only then that she realised she was injured – there was a sharp pain in her chest and arm. As she lost consciousness she dimly heard a police siren in the distance.

As well as the serious danger, it is characteristic of the traumatic event that too much is happening too quickly for the brain to be able to process it – *information overload*. This will have repercussions later, as the brain has to rerun the events again and again in order to make sense of them and to work through all the implications.

'UNEVENTFUL' CRISIS

So far we have been examining crises which are triggered by a single, very stressful event which has massive threatening implications. Many crises are not like this. They are the result of a gradual build-up of stress, and the final crisis can be caused by something relatively trivial. The triggering factor is 'the last straw' rather than a particularly stressful event in itself – normally the person would take it in his or her stride. In an important sense these crises are 'uneventful', as they are not directly attributable to a single stressful experience. Here is an example:

❑ *Ben Martin couldn't remember when he had last enjoyed a day's work. His job as a community psychiatric nurse seemed to become more and more difficult instead of easier. For weeks now, getting up and leaving the house for work had been like putting on a heavy, damp overcoat. He felt more and more miserable as he approached his office, knowing he would find a new pile of casenotes and several phone messages on top of his already chaotic desk. Everyone was asking him to do something; always more demands. He never seemed to get on top if it. In fact it seemed to take him longer to do things than it took his colleagues. Recently he'd given up trying to keep proper notes, and he realised that there were a number of jobs he hadn't attended to. If he had a chance he went home early, but only spent the time drinking and watching television. He often went to the pub at lunch-time. One of the nurses he worked with, Karen, had asked if she could help, but there was something in her voice that made him feel she was criticising him – he'd nearly bitten her head off, saying very abruptly that he was fine, thanks, and that she should worry about her own work.*

One day he made a visit to a woman who was suffering dementia. She was confused, thought she was being poisoned, kept trying to leave the house. She wouldn't let her husband or him near her to wash or feed her and she wouldn't stay in bed at night. Ben felt the situation at home had become impossible and that she should be admitted to hospital. He made the arrangements, but the consultant psychiatrist could not be found, so the junior doctor and he completed the admission procedure. The next day the consultant walked into his office without knocking. He was very annoyed that Ben had taken it on himself to admit the woman, and asked what he thought he was doing: 'You can hardly manage to do your own job without trying to do mine.' Ben felt himself lose control as he raised his voice at the consultant, who also started shouting. Ben stood up and lashed out at the psychiatrist, yelling 'Get out of my room you bastard!' It was only when he saw that the doctor had been knocked off balance and was sprawled on the floor clutching his face that Ben realised he was in big trouble.

You could argue that Ben has created his own crisis by his earlier choices in responding to work difficulties. Almost every member of the caring professions experiences work overload from time to time. For some reason, Ben is more vulnerable to this kind of stress than many others. No two people respond identically to the same situation. Ben has been putting off action, and instead of doing anything about it has been trying to push the reality of his problem away by cutting off from his job, by avoiding work and by drinking. You could even see the crisis as a result of Ben's way of pushing things to the limit, which eventually provokes a critical situation. Without realising what we are doing, we can often create a crisis by forcing matters to a head. It is as if we are hoping, deep down, for someone to recognise the mess we are in and help us. In this sense a crisis can contain a *hidden communication* about a long-standing personal difficulty and what is needed to resolve it.

WHAT A CRISIS IS NOT

Finally, it is worth thinking about non-critical situations which might be mistaken for crises. There are important distinctions to be drawn if we are not to make an inappropriate intervention.

The common features of crisis are summarised in Box 1.1.

BOX 1.1 Defining features of crisis

- a triggering stress event or long-term stress

- the individual experiences distress

- there is loss, danger, or humiliation

- there is a sense of uncontrollability

- the events feel unexpected

- there is disruption of routine

- there is uncertainty about the future

- the distress continues over time (from about two to six weeks)

If these features are present, there is a high probability that you are dealing with a crisis; but if they are not, be careful. Two situations can mimic crisis. First, where there has been a stressful event. Stress, even severe stress, is not equivalent to crisis if the person does not experience it as uncontrollable. For example, someone could be aware they are under stress and so have mobilised adequate personal and social resources to deal with it. The other situation is where someone is very upset at a particular moment without any evidence of an underlying stressful event of any kind. It is easy to be carried along with someone's feelings and be led into thinking they are facing a major crisis when it is simply that you have caught them at an emotionally vulnerable moment, perhaps due to tiredness or illness. The next morning, things might look completely different. A crisis is not a one- or two-day affair but holds long-term threat and does not usually resolve within two weeks.

This chapter has reviewed a range of different types of crisis. In order to establish the defining features of crisis, I have deliberately chosen simple examples. You may well be feeling that they are too straightforward compared to some of the crises you have to deal with. Of course, professional workers tend to see multifaceted crises involving a series of interrelated events and long-standing personal difficulties which are hard to untangle. This is partly because straightforward crisis is often contained within a natural support system, without the need for professional involvement.

Apart from their great complexity, there is nothing different about these multifaceted crises. All the elements of simpler crises will be present – loss, danger, negative revelation, humiliation, uncontrollability, disruption of routine, uncertainty, hidden communication – and the first task is to unravel them. Begin by completing Exercise 2. Following Chapter 3, there is a case history as a further exercise in understanding complex crisis.

ANALYSING A CRISIS

EXERCISE 2

To complete this exercise you will need a pen and paper. First, think about a crisis, preferably a personal crisis, you have undergone. This may be recently or in the past. You can also think about someone else's crisis with which you have been personally involved, but this is less informative. To explore what kind of crisis this was, write down your answers to the following questions.

? What was the event or difficulty which triggered the crisis? Describe what happened.

? Were there any background features which made this event particularly difficult at that time? Describe the context in which it occurred.

? Was the crisis unexpected? How much warning did you have that things were going to go wrong? Looking back, was there anything you could have done to prevent it?

? Once the crisis occurred, how much control over events did you feel you had? Looking back, was this assessment realistic?

? To what extent did your routine change as a result of this crisis? Note any disruption to regular patterns of work/leisure, sleeping/ waking, seeing different people.

? At the beginning of the crisis, how much uncertainty was there about the outcome? Was it possible for you to predict what might happen in the future? If not, why not?

? Did the crisis involve any personal loss? If so, what kind of loss (examples include loss of a loved person through death, other loss of a relationship, loss of a valued ideal, loss of status, loss of independence, loss of bodily function)? Describe what the loss meant to you.

? Did the crisis involve any threat or danger? If so, describe this.

? Was there any humiliation involved in the crisis? Try to explain exactly what you found humiliating.

? Was there any element of negative revelation – finding out something upsetting you did not previously know about?

? Looking back, can you see if there might have been a hidden communication in your crisis? What was the crisis saying about you and the way your life was developing at that time?

Chapter Two

How Do People Respond To Crisis?

We have already seen some of the immediate effects of severe stress. Remember Jill trying to help her friend after the motorway accident? She felt completely unreal – as if she were watching a film or dreaming. This sense of floating unreality is an invariable response to really frightening things. Notice also that Jill, although badly hurt, was completely unaware of her injuries until her legs gave way. This reaction is built into our bodily mechanisms. In response to trauma the body produces chemicals which are natural painkillers and tranquillisers. It is easy to see that this form of anaesthesia has a purpose. It protects us physically and mentally from the disabling effects of being overwhelmed by pain or fear. It can give a kind of cold detachment, so that it is possible to act calmly and rationally. It is a way of 'buying time' to deal with the external threat. The intense form of detachment is seen in severe stress, but to a lesser degree it could be a feature of any crisis.

This deadening of feeling is temporary, and later there is emotional and physical turmoil. Sleep patterns are disrupted. Often it is difficult to fall asleep at night due to thoughts going round and round. Sometimes people can get to sleep all right but wake frequently during the night. Even an apparently ordinary night's sleep may not be refreshing – without knowing it, the person has been tossing and turning, calling out or grinding teeth. Little wonder that one can wake up exhausted from such tension. Normal appetite and digestion are also disrupted. Other signs of crisis are a physical tiredness even if one has not been working particularly hard, an apathetic, slowed-down feeling, tension in the muscles and pain due to this tension – often headaches but also pain in the back, neck and shoulders.

Some people respond to stress with physical illness rather than psychological problems (although the two are not incompatible!). For example, a bad back, gynaecological pain, chest pain, eczema and colitis can all flare up in response to a crisis. Furthermore, stress may interfere with the body's natural defences against disease – the immune system – making one more likely to end up in bed with flu or glandular fever.

ANXIETY

A fundamental component of crisis is *anxiety*. This has a physical as well as a psychological dimension. When we perceive threat or danger, chemicals are released into the bloodstream which have dramatic effects. The heart beats faster and more strongly. Blood supply is diverted from digestion and other routine tasks and redirected to the muscles. Blood composition changes so that it clots more easily and more oxygen is taken in. The point of all this is to prepare us to face an attack, or to run away from it, and to do so with more strength and speed than we could normally muster. Now this is all very well for wild animals, but for most threatening situations humans are faced with in modern life, it just isn't possible either to fight back or to run away. Our crises are more complex than the animal's confrontation with a hungry predator. When the body gets itself geared up for a massive burst of effort, but nothing happens, it can produce problems. What's more, for humans, anxiety does not begin and end with physical events. We have the added problem of thinking.

Let's pick up the story of George Dee, the redundant manager, a week after he received the news of being sacked.

❑ *George slept badly. He fell asleep all right but then woke up suddenly, his heart racing, and had to sit up and put the light on. He settled down eventually, but slept fitfully. The next day he went into the office for the last time, to pick up his things and to say goodbye to one or two people. On the tube train he felt he couldn't get enough air to breathe properly. He began to sweat and feel trembly, as if his knees were going to give way. Feeling terribly ill, he left the train at the next stop and sat down on a seat on the platform. His head was swimming, his heart pounding – alarmingly, it seemed to miss a couple of beats. 'I'm having a heart attack', he thought.*

As you might imagine, George was not having a heart attack. He was having a panic attack. Most people do not realise how frightening and unpleasant this is, but it really felt to George as if he must be dying. What happened? The sacking has left his bodily defences alerted, 'all systems go' for a fight with the boss. A physical fight is out of the question. Nevertheless, his body is ready – fast heartbeat, adrenalin in his bloodstream. The problem gets out of control when he is in the train because his anxiety level starts to rise at the thought of saying goodbye to people in the office. Without realising it, he is breathing very fast and shallowly. In the absence of strenuous physical effort, this causes a physical reaction, a jittery, dizzy sensation. The anxiety produces more thoughts and images – these are flowing quickly and automatically th-ough his mind now – of collapsing in the train and everyone looking at him, of not being able to get out. These thoughts make him more anxious and he continues to gulp in air, which only increases the unpleasant dizzy feeling. By this time he thinks he is seriously ill, and the thought about the heart attack is guaranteed to make things worse.

All emotional reactions affect the way we think, and the way we think affects our emotions. High levels of anxiety colour our judgements, making it more likely that we will believe the frightening thoughts which normally we would be able to dismiss without difficulty. A similar process happens when we are depressed or angry. The thoughts which match the emotions carry weight with us – we are likely to believe them. This can set up a closed and vicious circle. In general, as we saw in Chapter 1, there is some triggering event which starts off the crisis. However, the real crisis only begins because of our responses to this event tipping things out of control. Sometimes it is the response to the initial event which causes all the trouble rather than the event itself, as we saw with Ben, the angry nurse.

One way or another, anxiety is pervasive in crisis. We can't help trying to avoid anxiety: in fact many of our mental processes are designed to do just this. In a strange way, though, during a crisis, when we cannot avoid feeling anxious, it is better to accept and tolerate anxiety without becoming frightened by it. This is a difficult skill to learn, but as we shall see later it is an important one, both for the person in the crisis and those wanting to help.

PROBLEMS WITH THINKING CLEARLY

Even those who avoid the vicious circle of anxiety about anxiety will find that the crisis has affected the efficiency of their thinking processes. Normally we take for granted our mind's ability to think something through, to make decisions, to concentrate attention on the task facing us. Only when this wonderful set of abilities breaks down to some extent can we appreciate how much we depend on them.

Making accurate judgements and reasoning things out is much more difficult for someone in a crisis. Strong emotions and mental preoccupation with the immediate issues reduce the capacity for thinking clearly. For example, the day after his arrest, Gerald wanted to resign his job, sell the house and move to another part of the country. It took a long discussion with his wife to convince him that this might not be the best way of dealing with the problem. His *poor judgement* about the consequences of his actions was caused by the stressful event. Taking impulsive action in the throes of a crisis often creates future problems. In people whose crises have developed slowly, like Ben the community nurse, judgement and reasoning are affected in another way. At some point along the road to crisis, these people lose the ability to judge the best way forward, not knowing, for example, when or how to ask for help. This result of their stress is, of course, guaranteed to intensify the crisis.

The effects on our mental processes are not confined to reasoning. A week after the event leading to his crisis, Gerald is still having trouble:

☐ *'For God's sake Gerald, answer me!' The sharpness of his wife's voice made him look up from his newspaper. 'I said do you mind if I go over to Mary's this morning?' Hastily reassuring her that he didn't mind, Gerald returned to the paper, but couldn't remember what he had been reading. He started on the letters page, which he normally enjoyed, but after the third attempt to read the first letter, he gave up. The words just didn't sink in. He decided to get started on papering the dining room. He had just finished pasting the first strip of wallpaper when the phone rang. It was a friend from the dramatic society asking if he was all right – they had been worried when he hadn't turned up the previous evening for the committee meeting. He apologised and made a quick excuse. Secretly he was appalled – he had completely forgotten about the meeting! How could he? He made a cup of tea and drifting into the garden, started to potter about. About an hour later he returned to the house and found, to his exasperation, a strip of pasted wallpaper – bone-dry. He had to start again.*

Gerald's capacity to respond to the routine demands of his environment is severely reduced during this crisis. Fortunately he is on holiday from running the school, so that his *absent-mindedness* and *loss of concentration* do not have serious effects. Sometimes, though, people in crisis continue attempting to tackle highly demanding and complex tasks, and then become depressed by their failure, seeing this as a sign of personal weakness. Again we see how people's thoughts about and reactions to the initial stress response can either help to resolve the crisis or intensify it. When things are bad, we often make them worse: it seems a cruel irony, but you can observe this happening again and again.

AVOIDANCE AND PREOCCUPATION

So far we have seen that, in general, acute stress causes a period of unreal detachment and all stress leads to raised levels of anxiety, which in turn causes sleep disturbance, physical symptoms and inability to think straight.

The first shock of the triggering event is over, but in a sense the crisis has only just begun. Depending on the nature of the event, a series of changes to the person's mental and emotional life take place. First, let's understand what is happening to Meg Brown, whose husband died so suddenly of heart failure.

☐ *A month after Jack's death, Meg still can't believe it. She remembers the ambulance men, the kindness of her neighbours, the funeral. She had many visitors, and then went to stay with her sister for a week. Now back in her own home, she keeps expecting to see Jack, expecting someone to come to the door and tell her it has all been a mistake. One evening, she found she had laid two places for supper. The next day, she heard Jack's voice, quite clearly, saying 'Meg?' just as he always used to when he first came home. She had the strangest feeling that he was going to walk in at any minute. She felt she had coped very well so far; everyone had told her she had been 'marvellous'. The only thing was, she couldn't cry and she couldn't bear anyone to mention Jack's name. One day, she was rushing to get ready to go down to the hospital where she helped out with the volunteers' shop. She opened her dressing-table drawer to find her scarf and, as she was rummaging, found one of Jack's handkerchiefs. As she held it, a tidal wave of pain, of desolate loss, washed over her body. She was hardly able to breathe and began to sob. Emptiness, longing, and a feeling of abandonment flooded through her. She couldn't stop crying for half an hour.*

The grief that Meg feels is delayed, but the feelings are perfectly normal. Grief is not an illness or a psychological problem; it is a way of working through the implications of loss, first by raising angry protest about the abandonment, next a constant search for the lost person, then desolate acceptance of the reality of the loss. These processes allow the final resolution of grief, enabling the bereaved person to move beyond it to take up the threads of life again, to form new attachments and to build a new identity.

Following bereavement, the mind has a great deal of work to do during the process of coming to terms with the new reality. Two very different things will happen, but in fact they are aspects of the same process. There will be moments of complete numbness, as if it has not happened – the unreal feeing. The person may try to avoid thinking or talking about the loss. Both consciously and unconsciously, there is an *avoidance* of the truth, and this can be seen as a long-term extension of the dream-like detachment immediately after the event. Alongside the avoidance, alternating with it, there is a *mental preoccupation* with the source of stress. Thoughts and memories will intrude themselves into the bereaved person's mind. These memories bring waves of strong feelings, as does anything that reminds the person of the reality of the death.

After traumatic stress, this preoccupation can take the form of *flashbacks*: involuntary reliving of the trauma through mental images. Flashbacks are extremely distressing, because fear rather than detachment is now experienced. We can return to Jill Black, who had this experience following the motorway pile-up.

❑ *Two days after the accident, Jill was discharged from the hospital with a broken arm, broken ribs, and bruises. Peggy had serious internal injuries and, after an operation, remained in hospital. Two close friends collected Jill from the hospital and ensured she had everything she needed at home. When they left, although it was still early, she decided to go straight to bed. As she lay down, she suddenly found herself seeing the accident again. She broke out in a sweat as she saw and felt herself hauling on the steering wheel and heard the sound of squealing tyres. Then there was a sickeningly vivid picture of Peggy, crushed and bleeding. Trembling and nauseous, Jill hurriedly leapt out of bed, wincing at the pain in her side, and went downstairs to make herself a drink and listen to some music.*

Re-experiencing seems to be an essential part of the mental processing of the event. It is not the start of breakdown but a sign that the mind is working hard to assimilate what has happened and to integrate it with previous experience. Dreams and nightmares about an accident or a death are related phenomena. Flashbacks to a trauma can be seen as an intense form of the preoccupation which is characteristic of all crisis.

These examples have something to teach us about all stress responses. You will find that the twin processes of avoidance and mental preoccupation, although they may seem contradictory, are almost always present during a crisis. It is certainly true for Janice Bowers after her husband's unwelcome revelation.

❑ *The week after Pete moved out, Janice found that she couldn't stop thinking about 'the other woman'. She found herself going over and over in her mind incidents which at the time she had not thought about – such as when the phone rang and someone at the other end put it down, or once when Pete had suddenly insisted they leave a friend's party, even though Janice was enjoying herself. Now she relived the last two years, reinterpreting events, with her mind returning to thoughts and images of Pete and his woman friend. Every time she thought about it, she felt terrible – there was a kind of burning, breathless feeling in her chest.*

Although she was torturing herself by going over and over it, she couldn't stop herself. Whatever she did to take her mind off it, she would soon find herself thinking about it again. She tried to talk to her mother, but it was difficult since she took the attitude, 'You're well rid of him – he never did you any good.' Janice began to avoid going out whenever possible, believing that people were looking at her and talking about what had happened. She dreaded going anywhere that she might possibly see Pete, and often thought about this happening and how dreadful it would be.

Janice is in the grip of a thought process she cannot easily control. This form of mental preoccupation is sometimes called 'ruminating' and is common in crises stemming from negative revelation. It causes great distress, yet continues despite the person's attempts to push the thoughts away. Each bout of thinking sets off anxiety. As distress increases, further horrible thoughts crowd in. In Janice's case, these thoughts are that she is the object off sneering and belittling gossip in the neighbourhood, that it would be catastrophic to come across Pete accidentally, that every positive or affectionate thing Pete did is now shown to be completely false, that he and his woman had been laughing and enjoying themselves whilst she was working hard at home. There is no end to the stream of thoughts; and the more she tries to stop thinking about it, the more intrusive they become.

BEHAVIOUR CHANGE

Note how, for Janice, the thoughts and distress lead to avoidance in the form of *changes in behaviour*. Janice starts to withdraw from her usual routine and from any social contact. Her response to the crisis is pushing her away from distraction, enjoyment or other resources and further into isolation. This in turn makes the ruminating thoughts more frequent and intense.

Behaviour changes frequently occur during crisis. They include social withdrawal and giving up previous enjoyable activities. Drug use is common – alcohol, of course, but also other drugs such as Valium (diazepam) or painkillers like aspirin and paracetamol. Often these changes are serving to protect the victim from the source of pain. They may be necessary for the short term, but they are rarely successful or helpful in the long term.

DEPRESSION

Janice is also *depressed* – another emotion produced by crises, particularly those involving loss or humiliation. The signs of depression are a low, miserable mood which may include weeping; loss of interest in the outside world; feeling tired and apathetic – nothing seems worth the effort. In particular, there is an all-pervasive negative view of oneself and other people. The goodness drains out of the world. Everything seems bleak and hopeless, and there may not seem to be any point in continued existence.

Depressed mood may turn into a depressive disorder if the crisis is not resolved positively. Here the mood state is severe and hardly varies. There is continued sleep disturbance, brooding, loss of appetite, suicidal thoughts, and the person becomes slow to do things or to respond when spoken to. In very severe depression the person may develop delusional ideas: for example, that she is guilty of unforgivable sin, or that his internal body organs are rotten and stinking. Clinical depression is a serious and life-threatening problem, so that ways of preventing it are extremely important.

As in anxiety, thoughts and beliefs play an important part in the development of depression. Negative thoughts automatically pop into the mind of the depressed person. You have probably noticed this yourself. When we feel miserable, all kinds of horrible ideas come into our minds. Here are some examples of common ones (see if you recognise them): 'I'm looking old and unattractive'; 'My relationship is a disaster, we don't really love each other'; 'That piece of work I did is really no good at all'. The more depressed we are, the more likely we are to believe these ideas. It is harder to remember any evidence to contradict them, because our memory processes are also affected by mood: in depression, one remembers negative experiences and it is hard to gain access to positive memories. When we feel better, which for many of us might be the next morning, we can see that we had it out of proportion. For some people, however, this recovery does not occur, and the negative thoughts serve to deepen the depression. Certain deeply-rooted beliefs about oneself and the way things are, ways of seeing things which are learned from childhood experiences, can make it more likely that the thoughts are not dismissed. (We shall examine these beliefs in more detail in the next chapter.) This seems to be one way that, for some people, a natural depression in response to crisis does not lift as the person regains equilibrium, but instead spirals into an episode of prolonged and severe distress.

OTHER POWERFUL EMOTIONS

We have seen how anxiety, intrusive thoughts, avoidance and depression are all possible responses to crisis. *Anger, guilt* and *shame* are three other closely related emotions.

ANGER

Anger stems from a sense of grievance. Remember Ben's irritation at Karen's offer of help, and his later rage at the consultant's rudeness and arrogance? His work stress affected him by making him feel aggressive (in someone else it could have led to anxiety or depression) and, in combination with the large amounts of alcohol he had been drinking, this led him to become physically violent. Ben was quite familiar with his colleague's high-handed behaviour, and in the past had silently fumed without showing his annoyance. Because Ben was already feeling at the end of his tether, because he had honestly done his best in making a difficult decision in an urgent situation, because he so desperately needed some support – all these factors added to his sense of grievance. Who knows, if the consultant had behaved courteously the crisis might have been temporarily averted.

It is important to note that the angry person's sense of grievance is ultimately generated not by the situation itself but by how he or she sees the situation. Given the same external trigger, whether a grievance is perceived will vary from person to person and, within the same person, from one occasion to another. Even if the person does feel aggrieved, whether an angry feeling leads to angry words and actions will also depend on the individual in a specific situation.

Anger is a misunderstood emotion, in that people tend to be either frightened of it or dominated by it, and in both cases think of it as 'a bad thing'. In fact, angry impulses are a normal response to frustration and a way of telling us that something is threatening us unjustly and we want to change things. Again, as with other powerful emotions like anxiety and depression, when anger is implicated in a crisis there is the possibility of things accelerating from bad to worse. For a start, anger is self-perpetuating. You may have noticed that there is no point arguing with an angry person, trying to get him or her to see your point of view. Seeing someone else's point of view is almost impossible when one is angry; the angry person can only see evidence which is consistent with the emotion. Besides, when we feel angry we do not want to stop feeling angry, we do not want to be mollified; we want to feel justified, and we will bend things until they seem to us to give further cause for anger. If, as in Ben's case, the anger leads to violence, it provides a short-term release of tension but it deepens the crisis.

Controlling (I prefer the term 'containing') anger is also widely misunderstood. It does not mean never *feeling* angry. There is not much wisdom in this – sometimes anger is an appropriate emotion. Someone who can never feel angry when faced with frustration, injustice or cruelty may become depressed and helpless, or physically ill instead. One could argue that this person has a problem with anger, no less than the one who flares up at the slightest provocation and throws rageful tantrums. Both are unable to tolerate the emotion and allow themselves actually to *feel* it – each is trying to avoid the feeling, either by discharging it or by repressing it. Both are failing to 'own' it as their feeling, their responsibility.

How often have you heard, or said, 'I'm sorry I did so-and-so but you made me lose my temper'? This implies that anger is one feeling for which we need take no responsibility and which excuses our actions. Some people create personal crises by their inability to contain anger without translating it into violence. Someone in this form of crisis can make a decision to take responsibility for it and can learn ways of preventing escalation.

Some people have jobs which tend to make them the target of people's anger: for example, police controlling a crowd, a social worker taking someone's child into care, or a middle manager trying to implement an unpopular policy decision from higher up. These roles are very stressful. Applying the principles outlined here would lead to an approach of containment rather than either appeasement or retaliation. The practicalities of working with anger in a crisis are discussed in Chapter 5.

In fact, almost any professional could find themselves caught up in an angry outburst. Anger is a thread woven through the fabric of many different types of crisis. In bereavement, for example, anger is aroused, and may be directed at medical and nursing staff, at friends or relatives, or towards God. Also, because of the abandonment, anger is often felt towards the person who died. Similarly, it is potentially involved in any crisis involving loss, humiliation or affront. In these situations, anger can sometimes be experienced as a substitute for more uncomfortable emotions such as fear, shame or guilt. The latter two are probably the least well understood of all emotions.

SHAME

Shame should not be confused with guilt. Gerald felt shame at having been arrested although he did not feel guilty. Shame is a negative form of self-consciousness where one feels like running away and hiding. It carries the sensation of being observed by a critical and unsympathetic judge who finds us wanting, contemptible or even disgusting. The trouble is that we ourselves are the judge; we can hardly bear ourselves.

Ironically, shame is commonly felt by people who have been victims of violence. Children who have been sexually abused, for example, feel shame at what has happened, as do rape victims. However irrational it may seem, this is a normal response. The victim's shame is one factor which makes it particularly dificult for them to find effective help within their existing social network. The shame felt by the victim is mirrored in other people's tendency to blame them. This has been shown to happen repeatedly: without meaning to, we tend to see victims as somehow responsible for their fate. Even if we do not assign blame, we find victims embarrassing. This is because, for our own peace of mind, we are striving to maintain the illusion that we are living in a just world where people more or less get what they deserve. The idea of *innocent victims* flies in the face of that belief and, in order to protect it, we find ourselves ready to blame them. In this sense, the victim's shame is consistent with his or her own belief in a just world, and it takes time to work through to a different belief.

GUILT

Guilt, on the other hand, is a feeling of moral responsibility for some bad action which hurts or damages another. Guilt often seems irrational to someone outside the crisis. For example, Meg Brown's guilt seems unbelievable to us, but is very real to her.

■ *Meg felt she should be starting to feel better; after all, it was nearly three months since the dreadful day Jack died. Funnily enough, sometimes it seemed like yesterday and at other times it seemed as if she had lived ten years without him. The long, dark, wakeful nights were the worst. There was a horrible secret which she had never mentioned to anyone, and the thought of it wouldn't let her rest. Whenever she remembered it, the colour went out of the day and a horror of what she had done came back. The thought had many guises, but basically boiled down to this: 'If I had fetched the towels when he asked for them, he would still be alive today.' Although she told no one, she couldn't stop blaming herself for his death. She felt remorse, and had lost track of the number of times she had said to herself 'if only . . . ' She reached the point of feeling that, in a way, she had killed him.*

We talk of such guilt as 'irrational', and in one sense it is, because entirely out of proportion to reality. But at a deeper level, guilt is often rooted in an angry or selfish impulse which might have caused harm if acted upon. For example, like many other couples, Meg and Jack had some painful areas in their marriage. One of the things Meg had always felt annoyed about was the way Jack depended on her to do things for him all the time. When Jack asked for the towels for the last time, Meg had a flash of anger – all her sense of being used and exploited welled up.

Right in the back of her mind she had a thought such as 'Oh get lost!', or even something stronger. Feeling impulses of hate and rage towards a loved one is a commonplace part of intimacy, and one of the challenges of close relationships is to integrate these with our love so that we can accept the other person more as they really are and less as we believe they should be. Some guilt is therefore a normal part of the bereavement response, but extreme guilt following a loss is a sign that something is wrong in the grieving process.

Guilt is very commonly reported by those who survive a disaster where others have perished. There is a powerful natural impulse to cling to life, even at the cost of someone else's, and the unconscious pleasure and relief at being alive can seem to be at someone else's expense. This may be at the root of survivors feeling guilty and unworthy of being alive.

Box 2.1 Responses to crisis stress

- Short-term unreality and anaesthesia

- Sleep disturbance

- Disrupted appetite and digestion

- Muscle tension

- Aches, pains, skin rashes, infections

- Anxiety and depression

- Problems with reasoning, judgement and concentration

- Avoidance of the problem (by thoughts and actions)

- Mental preoccupation with the problem

- Anger, shame and guilt

SEVERITY OF THE CRISIS RESPONSE

The responses to crisis are summarised in Box 2.1. They vary a great deal in their intensity. Some reactions are relatively mild and short-lived. Other people suffer intense responses which endure for months or even years. These variations in stress response reflect both individual factors, like personality, attitudes and coping styles, and social circumstances, such as financial resources or the availability of support from friends and relatives. The importance of the individual factors will be discussed in the next chapter, and the role of social networks in Chapter 5. Here I shall discuss those features of the crisis itself which are more likely to lead to difficult and prolonged stress reactions.

Bereavement is a severely stressful event, especially when it is the death of a spouse or a child; when the death is unexpected, sudden, or violent; or where no body is found. A family member is murdered or commits suicide; a child goes missing but is never found. It is very difficult to grieve these forms of loss.

Bereavement is also more likely to cause prolonged or intense reactions when the relationship with the lost person was particularly ambivalent, with strong positive and negative feelings mixed together. If a relationship is in difficulties when the death occurs, this leaves 'unfinished business' which again makes the process of grieving more complicated, with a greater likelihood of guilt or mental refusal to accept the reality of the loss.

Bereavement can cause special problems if the survivor was very dependent on the lost person for all their emotional and practical needs. Some people build their whole lives around one person, having no intimate friends and no independent skills. Loss of this person requires massive readjustment, which can be very slow or difficult.

Multiple crisis is unfortunately quite common, and is likely to cause severe problems. Before the process of accommodating to the first stressor has been completed, a further crisis arises to tax resources which are already severely depleted. A woman loses her husband, then within two months her son has his legs crushed in a road accident. A man loses his job, then his wife develops cancer. A woman loses her husband and mother within the same week, and six months later is raped. These tragic multiple events do not inevitably lead to psychological disorders, but are more likely to do so than a single crisis.

Traumatic stress produces more severe responses than other types of stress, for example, when many people die, particularly in horrifying circumstances and when the person witnessed violent death, injury or suffering. The reason why major disasters produce such intense stress is partly due to the high probability of sudden, violent bereavement, multiple loss and trauma. There is another factor in disasters. They demonstrate not only our own individual fallibility but the inability of society as a whole to prevent these tragedies. When a tube station or a football stadium catches fire, when a train or a plane crashes, an important illusion is damaged. The illusion is that even if I personally make mistakes and take responsibility for them, I can trust 'them' – the others, the people in authority whose job it is to run things – to take care of me and to make sure I am safe. It is deeply disturbing to discover that 'they' are human and are no more infallible than I am. This is why such disasters cause more fear, sadness and even outrage than the appalling annual statistics on death through road accidents or preventable diseases. Finally, there is a very special kind of stress caused by direct contact with the madness of arbitrary mass killing such as at Hungerford. The darkest side of our capacity for treating others as objects with no feelings is brought home to us – not in the torture chambers of some far-off country, not the cruelty described in history books, not horror during war when we have an 'enemy'. Human evil is brought into everyday life. This is truly terrifying.

This chapter has concentrated on the negative side of crisis. In particular I have tried to show how easy it is for the crisis to be intensified, or even created, by the individual's emotional response. When this is understood, one vital point becomes very clear. *Half of the skill of successfully working through crisis is not to make things worse than they already are.* The practical implications of this point are examined in Chapters 4, 5 and 6.

YOUR CHARACTERISTIC RESPONSE TO CRISIS

EXERCISE 3

Continue to work on the crisis you wrote about in Exercise 2 in the following way. Tick all the items which applied to you during the crisis.

I had difficulty sleeping as well as usual. ☐ ☐

Thoughts about the problem went round and round in my mind and I couldn't stop them. ☐ ☐

At times, I felt there was no point in going on. ☐ ☐

Looking back, I now see I had blown certain things up out of proportion and was not seeing them clearly. ☐ ☐

I suffered aches and pains or fell ill. ☐ ☐

I wanted to avoid seeing people and tried to be alone. ☐ ☐

I realise now I was drinking more than was good for me. ☐ ☐

At times, my heart beat faster than usual. ☐ ☐

There were times when I couldn't breathe properly. ☐ ☐

At times it felt as if it wasn't real. ☐ ☐

I was so wrapped up with my emotions it made things worse. ☐ ☐

I couldn't concentrate properly on my work. ☐ ☐

I became very irritable with people close to me. ☐ ☐

These are your responses to this particular crisis. Now repeat the exercise, ticking only those which are *characteristic* of your response to crisis – for example, on this particular occasion you may have felt anxiety, but it was an unusual feeling for you. On the other hand, being irritable could be a familiar and frequent feeling. Use the checklist to discover your own general style in responding to crises.

Chapter Three

Understanding Crisis

After defining crisis and spelling out different ways people respond, it is now time to go beneath the surface of human crisis, to understand what is happening at a psychological level and to discover the common threads in all crises, however superficially dissimilar they might seem. This leads to practical guidelines for working with crises which will be explored in later chapters. Although this chapter is more abstract and theoretical than the others, it explains some of the fundamental principles of a psychological approach to crisis. These principles are necessary to understand what one is doing and why.

It is sometimes difficult for people to see the importance of psychological factors when there may be genetic or biochemical processes involved, for example in emotions such as depression or anxiety. Sometimes people claim that depression is caused by biochemical changes in the body. Those who take this biomedical view speak as if physical phenomena were somehow more real than mental ones and had more power to explain things. Actually, even a thorough understanding of biological events would not take you very far in accounting for human emotions and behaviour.

Similarly, many 'caring professionals' believe that human problems are socially caused, by the life circumstances in which people find themselves and by the stress these produce. For example: 'Of course she's depressed – her husband has left her and she is living in poverty with two young children'. This is also inadequate to explain what happens in crisis, and if taken to an extreme leads to professional helplessness and pessimism. It is unhelpful to think about human experience in terms of only one type of cause having simple effects. Crisis is a meeting-point of many different influences. We must understand something about psychological processes as well as biological and social ones.

One important way of understanding crisis is to stop seeing human beings as 'objects' pushed, pulled and shaped by forces outside them (like heredity, poverty or stressful life events) and inside them (like hormones, memories or emotions). There is great value in seeing ourselves as active, if mostly unwitting, participants in constructing our everyday life stories. This is not a trivial point to be argued over by academics just for intellectual amusement. What you believe about this issue profoundly affects the way you will respond to crises – your own and other people's. Bear with me whilst I explain why I believe this *active construction* of our everyday reality is important.

CREATING OUR WORLD

It is a most extraordinary thing that although our eyes, ears, touch and other senses are simply picking up vibrations – light, sound, pressure – we seem to live in a solid world of people, objects and events. We have to organise and interpret those sensations to be able to decipher anything at all. This process of making sense of what is happening around us is fundamental. We don't need to think about it, any more than we need to think about digesting food in order to get nutrients into the bloodstream. Our digestion goes on working whether or not we think about it, and so do the processes of sensing, perceiving, attending, remembering, imagining, thinking and learning. It is very easy to take our everyday world for granted, just because it is so familiar and because we do not have access to the mysterious processes that make it possible.

Let's take a simple sequence of events: you are driving home from work, you pull up outside your house, you get out of the car, find your front-door key, and let yourself in. Just two minutes of straightforward routine which you have probably experienced hundreds of times without even being aware of it – nothing could be simpler. But it isn't simple at all. In order to achieve even this, thousands of complex mental procedures are combined in a miraculous way. You first have to know what a car is and how to drive it, a complex skill involving many finely-tuned judgements, correcting plans on the basis of new information and coordinating intentions and actions. You have to remember where you live and have a way of checking that you are on the right route. You will need an internal map or picture of what you expect to happen, otherwise you will fail to notice when things are not going according to plan. Throughout the drive, your brain and body get on with all this without your needing to pay conscious attention to it, leaving you free to think about what happened at work that day or what you intend to cook for dinner. When you do have to pay attention – when you are nearing the house and need to find the door key – you are brought back to the task. You are not distracted by the millions of other pieces of information which are bombarding your senses. In order to open the door, you must have formed a theory about how keys open doors. You don't throw it at the door, or slide it under the door – you fit it into the lock. If all this is involved in a simple routine task, it takes some imaginative effort to grasp all that is involved in processing information about the complex social order we inhabit.

In the social world of friends, neighbours, family, colleagues, we make many subtle judgements about others and their intentions – about intimacy, honesty, warmth, attraction, helpfulness and, most important, what the other person is thinking and feeling. A vast number of cues have to be interpreted and fitted into a theory which will make sense of the social acts we observe and in which we participate.

Alongside and interacting with all the processes so far mentioned are emotions. It is possible to think of emotions as an early-warning system that alerts us very quickly – much faster than conscious thought – to things which affect our personal welfare. By our emotional reactions we know that something 'out there' is threatening or benign, even before we know what it is or why it feels good or bad. This captures our attention and triggers the more discriminatory 'sense-making' of our reasoning and judgement. Of course, in complex human society, emotions are rarely pure and never simple – there is vast subtlety in emotional judgement. And emotions are not just biological events: they are intertwined with, even a product of, our language and social order. Consider the distinctions between guilt and shame, envy and jealousy, apprehension and foreboding. These emotions cannot be distinguished by recourse to biochemical studies of bodily events.

Now consider one of the most important facets of psychological reality. We have *selves*: that is, an 'I' which experiences being 'me' in relation to itself and others. To operate in the social world we must have an internal map or representation of this self, just as we must have a picture of how keys open doors to get inside our own homes. A large proportion of the mental and emotional life of most ordinary people is taken up with questions about the self. Am I loved? Am I safe? Am I approved of? Am I being made a fool of? What does so-and-so think of me? Much social information is screened and interpreted in terms of how it affects our view of ourselves. This applies to most of us far more than we would like to think, and we become even more aware of it when we are in psychological pain. I do not speak only of self-aggrandisement or self-love. Self-denial, self-denigration, self-depreciation, self-hatred are equally telling signs of this egocentric preoccupation.

We process information from the outside world via thought and emotion, and we judge much of that information on the self-protective criterion 'What does it say about me?' But in what sense do we 'construct' our reality? We are not simply matching information coming in from outside with pictures of the world that we have gained from past learning. We constantly strive to reduce the discrepancy between our theories of the world and the information we take in. Sometimes we do this by changing the internal picture, but just as often by interpreting everything in terms of it. In other words, what gets through and what is ignored depends on those internal pictures or beliefs. We often see what we expect or want to see. The way I see the world seems self-evident, as if that is the only possible way it could be; but nonetheless it is a construction, not a direct glimpse of a 'true reality'. Someone else could see it very differently, and might feel that *their* way was 'obviously' the way things really are.

Why is any of this important to an understanding of crisis? Quite simply because *crisis occurs when our theories about ourselves in relation to the outside world go fundamentally wrong*. It is not just about unpleasant things happening to us. It is certainly not just about our emotions going haywire or overwhelming us. In all crisis, the outside world (and that usually means other people) does not behave in the way we need it to: it refuses to confirm and validate our theories – and, most crucially, our theories about ourselves. It is as if your front door, one day, instead of opening when you turned the key, gave you an electric shock. Suddenly your theory about doors stops working properly.

PLANS THAT GO WRONG

Most crises are caused by one of three things. An important person fails to react in the way one expects; one's own body lets one down through illness or injury; or there is a massive disconfirmation of routine predictions, as in major disaster. Every individual has a mental plan for the future, a set of personal goals which give meaning and predictability to the world. Almost always, the realisation and confirmation of these plans depends on other people or on one's own body. When other people do not play the part that we have 'scripted' for them, our own identity is seriously damaged, and a similar thing happens when the body can no longer be relied upon. Besides, most bodily injury or illness will change the way people react to you. This is often one of the most difficult things about it.

Now we can see that, despite superficial differences, all the people whose lives we glimpsed in Chapters 1 and 2 have had similar underlying experiences. The crisis occurs because there is a sudden point at which, *in a fundamental way*, the individual's picture of the world, other people and the future no longer works. Sometimes the crisis does come 'out of the blue', as in Jill's accident or Helen's breast cancer. Here there is new information which by its very nature will be difficult to make sense of, and this takes some time. Even so, it is possible to resolve this type of crisis very successfully. Many women who have had breast cancer and surgery find that they have gained positive things from the experience, such as a sense of the value of life, or a feeling of being loved and valued as people respond to their needs. Here, faced with the task of making sense of something very threatening, there has been a change in the individual's theory about the world.

On the other hand, crises are often created by our own *reluctance* to change our theories. George and Ben are good examples of this. Their crises would have been averted if they had been able to adapt to a changing environment earlier. Why is it so difficult for us to do this? Often we take a view of ourselves and the world which is manifestly inadequate and leads to personal unhappiness, but we continue without learning from our experience and developing a better theory. The human capacity to cling to a way of seeing things which leads to self-destructive action is sometimes astonishing, even to those experienced in working with others. Often this is because something is blocking the new learning. When you get close to it, it is often because the person has a deep belief that the alternative *as he or she sees it* is utterly unacceptable – literally unbearable. George, for example, may have been working on this theory: 'Either I am very successful in my job or I will be utterly contemptible and despised'. When those are the only two choices you allow yourself, it does not leave much room to manoeuvre when things start to go wrong at work. There are other beliefs which, though relatively harmless in ordinary circumstances, can cause problems after a stressful event: the belief, for example, that it is virtuous to suffer, and that if you suffer enough you will be rewarded by being rescued by a perfect carer; the belief that you can only be valued if you try to please everyone all the time; the belief that fear can be overcome by avoiding contact with the source of fear.

'Well,' you might say, 'this doesn't sound so bad. Surely in a crisis people need to work out a new plan, a new set of personal goals, create a different picture of the world, one that works for the current situation.' Yes, but it isn't as simple as that. These plans and theories are not just like shopping lists, to be amended or discarded at will. Whilst we hold them, they *are* our reality. The collapse of one's reality is an extremely stressful process. You cannot take it in and believe it all at once. The mind goes on using the old plans, the old picture, and trying to make reality conform to it. This is what happens in bereavement. Meg Brown continued to experience the world as if Jack were still alive.

❏ *One evening, she found she had laid two places for supper. The next day, she heard Jack's voice, quite clearly, saying 'Meg?' just as he always used to when he first came home. She had the strangest feeling that he was going to walk in at any minute.*

Why does this invariably happen? Part of the reason is that any plan is better than no plan at all. One of the fundamental things about human beings is that we never give up trying to make sense of things – we just can't help doing it. We find meaninglessness intolerable. Similarly we veer away from a situation where there is no definition of 'self' – most people find the collapse of the self a terrifying experience. In crisis, by its very nature, it is not small adjustments to the picture that are needed, but in one way or another a fundamental rethink. This cannot be achieved all at once and painlessly.

Finally, the radical discrepancy between the internal picture of things and the messages coming from outside causes emotion. As we have seen, emotions are a valuable part of our finding out and responding to what's going on outside. They signal that something needs attention, though if very powerful can be difficult to handle. Even mild emotions are signals which, if ignored, can become a major problem. Generally, people tend to avoid emotional pain even when it would be wiser not to. Again and again we vote for the short-term relief of anxiety at the cost of a long-term solution to the problem. When the crisis finally hits us, what might have begun as apprehension, chagrin and sadness is now transformed into panic, rage and despair – a much less manageable proposition. When are are experiencing such powerful emotions, any new learning is very seriously impaired. That partly explains why it is sometimes so difficult to learn from experience, to build a new picture which works better. Often, instead of revising their understanding of themselves and the world, people in crisis cling to the old one, which seriously limits their potential and their future options.

All this happens without our realising it. We mistake our *picture* of ourselves and the world for the *reality* of the self and the world. We don't think of it as a picture: to us, it *is* reality. When the crisis occurs, we literally don't know what is happening because we don't have a picture of it. In a sense, all we know is where it hurts, where the reality has stopped fitting the picture. One way of working through crises is to grasp what part of our self-definition, our internal picture of the world in relation to us, has been damaged. This is a good first step towards acknowledging the problem and finding a way of building a new picture. Even if this rebuilding is not done *consciously* (and most people overestimate the power of the conscious mind in this respect), we *can* consciously create the conditions necessary for the *unconscious* part of the mind to work on the problem constructively. The next three chapters will describe practical ways of doing this.

In all the crises we have examined so far, there has been a fundamental challenge to the individuals' understanding of themselves in relation to external reality. It is possible to list the particular individual beliefs which are challenged or denied by these different crises. (see Box 3.1)

BOX 3.1 Summary of individual beliefs challenged by crises

Meg Brown	☐ Bereavement	Jack and I have a shared future.
Janice Bowers	☐ Revelation of marital infidelity	Pete loves me; I'm the most important person in his world.
Gerald White	☐ Arrest for shoplifting	I'm a respected member of my local community.
George Dee	☐ Getting the sack	I'm a valued employee.
Helen Smith	☐ Discovery of breast lump	I have a healthy, attractive body and a long (unlimited) future.
Paul Stanton	☐ AIDS diagnosis	I will not die young.
Jill Black	☐ Car accident	I am living in a safe world.
Ben Martin	☐ Attacking a colleague	I am in control of my life and can handle my work stress.

So: we start a crisis with reality giving us a metaphorical punch on the nose. We all have beliefs about ourselves and the world which sustain us, which allow us to feel safe and free to get on with life without fear or despair. When these core beliefs depend on either *other people* or *our own bodies* to be maintained, we are always potentially vulnerable, since it is in the nature of things that neither of these are utterly reliable and perfect. There is a constant possibility of our core beliefs being disconfirmed. However, while many people seem to go from one crisis to another, others seem to avoid crises altogether. Why should there be these differences between people?

LIVING WITHOUT CRISIS

One way to crisis-free living is to avoid being involved with others. Perhaps you know someone who cuts him- or herself off from other people, never becoming emotionally involved, never allowing any intimacy, never engaging in a competitive challenge, living in a private world? In this way they hope to avoid the pains of loss, of grief, of guilt, of fear. The price of such crisis avoidance is very high. There can be a core of loneliness which is a constant burden. Besides this, sooner or later, the threat of death will produce an ultimate challenge to the belief in invulnerability.

Different degrees of proneness to crisis could be a matter of chance. Perhaps some people are lucky. Even if unpleasant life events were handed out randomly, somebody would have to, so to speak, pick the short straw. This chance factor is an aspect of life which is often hard to accept. 'Why did it happen to me?' is the question everyone asks when they have suffered a terrible but chance event.

Of course, some people *are* 'lucky' in avoiding major illnesses or accidents. One paradox is that those who have been *un*lucky, who have been in an horrific disaster, are often aware that they could easily have died, and therefore feel obliged to be thankful for their 'good fortune'. As one Zeebrugge ferry survivor said: 'Everyone tells me how lucky I am. For weeks I kept agreeing, yes I'm really lucky. So why do I feel so terrible?' The truth is that this man was not 'lucky' at all, but tragically unlucky, and the denial of this by himself and others did not help him at all.

On the other hand, many crises arise from events which we ourselves influence – getting divorced or losing a job, for example. There is an element of luck here too, but much more scope for people to prevent the crisis. This is where an early grasp of what is happening, of the ways in which we are not in tune with the world outside, is so important.

By responding and adapting to early warnings, people adjust their view of the problem and can often take effective action. For example, Janice Bowers knew that she and Pete were not having any time together to talk through their private feelings and concerns. She feared confronting Pete with her needs, unsure of her right to do so, worried she was being unreasonable, frightened of hearing him reject her. Feeling unsure of her self-worth, she tried to protect herself by placating Pete and turning a blind eye to his neglect of her and their children. Ironically, this avoidance contributed to the very thing she dreaded and confirmed her picture of herself as powerless to control bad outcomes.

Many crises are preventable if we put our minds to it. Paying attention to emotional 'warning signs' gives us an opportunity to work out a strategy for coping so that we change course in time, preventing the need for a head-on collision with reality. Even better is to build crisis prevention into our lives so that we have a much better chance of keeping clear of problems. The key to crisis prevention is therefore planning ahead, foreseeing possible difficulties and acting early to take account of them. For example, a married couple approaching their retirement may have built up a wonderful future in their minds – moving to a small country cottage, growing flowers and vegetables, plenty of peace and quiet. This is fine, but the vision may be so compelling that they do not plan for all contingencies. Moving away from a tried and trusted network of friends, relatives and neighbours is in itself stressful, and it takes considerable time to build a new support system. Country cottages tend to be cut off from easy access to shops and medical services, making it essential to drive a car. The plan does not take account of what might happen in old age, when reduced income, illness, disability or bereavement all need to be considered.

Many people find the idea of individuals being responsible for constructing their own realities to be politically naïve, even dangerous. The argument here is that people are victims of unfair disadvantage. We know that life stresses are not randomly allocated and that those who are poor or stigmatised suffer a greater number of stressful events and difficulties than those who occupy roles of higher status. But does the vision of crisis described here imply a need to adjust to an unfair and oppressive reality? On the contrary, making sense of reality does not mean passively accepting another person's view of oneself, least of all a dominant orthodoxy about one's role or status. Understanding one's own part in constructing one's world is empowering, since it can free one to act effectively.

Although it is possible to prevent many crises, this does mean being prepared to learn from the experience of past crises. This learning can

UNDERSTANDING A COMPLEX CRISIS

EXERCISE 4

In this Exercise you have a chance to apply what you have read in Chapters 1, 2 and 3 to unravel and understand a realistically complex crisis. At this stage you are not attempting to work out what you should *do* about it. You are simply getting the anatomy of the crisis clear in your mind. Have pencil and paper ready to take notes. Read the vignette and then answer the questions.

☐ *A manager of a small industrial laboratory became concerned about one of the junior chemists. Usually very competent, for the past three months he had become unreliable in his timekeeping and was frequently absent. The manager thought that possibly something was wrong at home, but when he tried to talk about it, he met with a sullen response. One day, the manager suspected that the chemist was drunk and decided to check his work that evening – he found that over the past weeks the results of a number of tests had been falsified.*

Knowing that things were moving towards a dismissal, he called the chemist into his office and confronted him. The man first of all denied the faking and said he didn't know why he had been ill a lot recently. When the manager persisted, he became angry and nearly stormed out of the office. The manager reminded him that they were talking about the possibility of his being sacked. Soon after this the chemist became silent and the manager just waited for him to speak. He finally broke down in tears and began to talk rather incoherently. It took the manager a long time to piece together the following account.

Gambling had been a longstanding passion for the chemist but over the past year had become a serious problem. He had suffered several losses and was quite deeply in debt but had managed to keep this information from his wife. He was determined not to upset her because three months ago she had given birth to their first child prematurely and it was being cared for in hopsital. On top of this, his mother died suddenly from a stroke two weeks after the birth, never having seen her grandchild. Then he received a letter threatening legal proceedings from one of his creditors. Feeling desperate, he had stolen cash from his wife's sister in order to bet on a 'certainty'. Instead he had lost the money and eventually his wife and her family had become involved. There had been some very angry scenes during one of which he had physically fought with his wife's brother-in-law. Now he was estranged from his wife and was living alone, trying to sort out the debts but finding it very difficult. Over the past month he had been unable to concentrate on his work and was drinking. He knew he was in danger of losing his job and had been copying data from old tests in order to buy himself time to sort things out. He felt that if he lost this job, it would be the end of him.

After this confession the manager felt moved but also quite confused and, for some reason, rather annoyed. He advised the man to go home and to take a couple of days off sick to get some rest. He arranged to see him to discuss things on the third day, promising that he would take no action until then.

The manager feels overwhelmed by all this information. If you were in his shoes how would you begin to sort it out?

1. Make a list of all the *stress events* in the chemist's life. It does not matter at this stage whether they arise from his own actions or not.

2. For each stressor separately answer the following questions:

▶ Was there loss involved? If so, what was lost?

▶ Was there danger?

▶ Was there any humiliation?

▶ How uncontrollable do you think the event felt to the chemist?

▶ How unexpected was the event?

▶ Did it involve disruption of routine?

▶ How much uncertainty about the future was involved?

3. Were these events related to each other? Work out the sequence (i.e. which caused the next) and which were independent.

4. For each stress event, try to sketch out which core belief about himself and others is being challenged. (see Chapter 3)

5. For the crisis as a whole, make a list of the chemist's physical, emotional and behavioural responses. (If necessary, refer back to Chapter 2 to remind you of these.)

6. Finally, go back to the list of stress events and note those which were most likely caused by the chemist's own responses (noted above).

This kind of analysis does not have cut-and-dried answers which are either right or wrong, but you may find it interesting to compare your answers with mine (see page 112). You have now taken the first step in effective crisis work, which is to stop and think about exactly what is happening. It is important always to take the time to do this before rushing in to act. The next three chapters focus on the practicalities of how people can be helped to cope well with crisis and to work towards a constructive resolution. Following Chapter 6, we shall return to this example to apply these practical helping guidelines.

hurt. It can hurt to the point where we prefer not to do it, where we prefer just to keep our fingers crossed that things will turn out better next time. Sometimes they do – we get away with it. Often they don't. The next husband turns out to be an alcoholic bully like the last one. The next job turns out to have the same difficulties, the same unmanageable demands. Somehow or other, our good intentions are not realised and a repetitive pattern is established.

On the positive side, people often learn a great deal from crisis. This is the sense in which crisis is an opportunity for personal development. If the core belief is revised, a deeper and better understanding of oneself and the world results. The pain is therefore not pointless but more like the pain of giving birth – something new and good emerges. The time of crisis is a decisive moment, as implied, by the Greek root *krisis* (from *krinein*, to decide). By definition, we are in touch with a way in which our view of things has failed to take account of reality. In one sense, the decision is whether to defend that view against any evidence or to develop a different one. As I have implied, the choice does not depend on a merely *rational* decision-making process, but one which engages the whole person, on every level of consciousness. Here it is vital to be able to bear emotional pain in order to learn something useful from the experience.

At this point you may be feeling that you have a basic grasp of the psychology of crisis. You may find it useful to see how these ideas can be applied to a more complex example of a crisis situation. Exercise 4 gives practice in unravelling the strands of a multifaceted crisis.

In the chapters which follow I shall give detailed attention to practical ways of working with crisis. These methods are not based on the assumption that it is important simply to get rid of the pain and put the crisis behind you, returning to 'normal' in the sense of restoring the status quo. The importance of coping strategies (Chapter 4), helping and being helped (Chapter 5) and managing stress (Chapter 6) is not that they push away the problem but that they provide ways of making the emotional pain bearable, so that new learning can take place. The long-term effects of crisis (Chapter 7) depend on exactly this. If this book has a message, it is that we can make crisis *meaningful*, so that from being passive victims, dumb suffering animals, we can become active learners, fully human.

Chapter Four

Coping Skills

So far, although I have claimed that people in crisis do not have to be passive victims, I have not examined how people manage the unmanageable. The term *coping* describes all the ways individuals go about mastering or assuaging the stress which results when events challenge their routine predictions about the world. By studying these coping responses in detail, we learn about a broad repertoire of such skills. This is valuable both to those who are suffering a crisis and to the people helping them.

Although there are many different coping responses to crisis, they can all be summarised under two broad headings: coping with the *feelings*, or coping with the *problem*. Of course, this neat conceptual division is made for our own convenience in understanding such a variety of coping responses. In reality it is quite possible to tackle the crisis directly and at the same time regulate the feelings. Furthermore, no single coping strategy is the right one for all people in all situations. For example, there is some evidence that problem-focused coping is more effective in job crises than domestic ones, but even this does not apply to all individuals.

COPING WITH THE FEELINGS

It will be clear that the crisis has produced very intense and disruptive feelings. Not only are these intrinsically and acutely uncomfortable but, as we have seen, failure to cope with them causes the crisis to intensify. Finding the capacity to bear these feelings is a central part of coping. By coping with the feelings, vicious circles, where anxiety fuels panic or depression fuels despair, can be avoided. This is particularly true when the crisis is of a type beyond our control, where there is not much we can do to change things. In these circumstances, focusing one's coping efforts on the emotions makes good sense, although not all ways of doing so are equally effective.

One relatively ineffective way of trying to deal with painful feelings is by *wishful thinking*, almost attempting to undo what has happened. Such thoughts often start with 'If only . . . ' or 'I wish it were not true . . . ' People often become drawn into lengthy fantasies about what might have happened, what should have happened, and how it could all be so different – if only . . . This is a palliative coping method, for a short time evading the pain of truth, but it has the obvious drawback that no amount or intensity of longing is going to alter the facts. Sooner or later the cruel reality will return, with the added cruelty that one is no further forward in making sense of it. The dreaded future is still there, and time which could have been used to find new ways of facing it has been wasted.

Another palliative response which has considerable drawbacks is to use *drugs* to evade the pain. Many people in crisis consume substances such as alcohol, caffeine, nicotine, painkillers, tranquillisers, sleeping pills and antidepressants. Because these all interfere with the bio-chemistry of emotion, there are considerable dangers in their use during crisis, when the self-regulation of natural emotional response is needed to promote new learning and healing. In my experience, some drugs can contribute to a delay in this process to a point where psychological reconstruction becomes much more difficult. Many substances eventually cause psychological problems directly. For example, long-term over-use of caffeine produces anxiety symptoms, and withdrawal from the benzodiazepines (a chemical family of tranquillisers) can also replicate severe anxiety disorder. Alcohol can lead to the loss of social inhibitions. For example, the internal restraint which prevents us translating a violent impulse into a violent act can be lost, resulting in injury to oneself or someone else. Furthermore, a proportion of people will become dependent on the drug or start to abuse it. Abuse of any drug adversely affects mental processes which are already impaired by stress and intense emotion. Judgement, planning, reasoning and concentration are at a premium during the problem-solving part of a crisis, so it is unwise to reduce one's abilities still further. Because of the risk of dependency, any drug, whether medically prescribed or self-administered, should be used with extreme care during a crisis. There may be a role for their short-term use, for example to break a cycle of sleeplessness, but not as a substitute for other, more lasting help. Indeed, I would argue that there are many safer, and in the long run more effective, methods of coping with the emotional turmoil of a crisis.

Emotion-focused coping includes other ways of avoiding the pain, through either *suppression* or *distraction*. These give a break from the distressing thoughts and feelings, and buy time for the individual to begin the process of reconstructing their inner world. Suppression is partly automatic, but can be aided by a conscious act of will, along the lines of 'Just don't think about it; think about something else.' Distraction involves activity, keeping busy, doing things, so that one can concentrate on the task in hand rather than the feelings. This kind of activity, aimed mainly at keeping one's mind off the painful reality, should not be confused with the action-based coping methods discussed later. It is activity for its own sake, rather than with a particular problem-solving goal.

There is a definite place for suppression and distraction, especially in the early phases of the crisis. After all, we saw in Chapter 1 that a certain numbness and unreality are absolutely normal reactions, allowing someone who would otherwise be disabled by mental pain to function in the short term so they can gain a place of safety. Thus avoidance has a natural role to play. However, if it is the only or the main coping technique used it leads to problems. This is because, fundamentally, it is pushing away the feelings, and taken to an extreme this interferes with the reconstruction process. From the argument in Chapter 3 it is easy to see why this is. Emotions are giving absolutely vital information about where exactly there is a mismatch between one's constructed world and the real world. This information must not be ignored if new learning is to take place.

The other problem with distraction is that it often just doesn't work very well. There comes a point where the emotional reaction will come flooding in, however assiduously one is trying to keep busy. Remember Meg Brown, whose husband died so suddenly? She was using distraction a great deal, and thought she was doing pretty well, until . . .

☐ *One day, she was rushing to get ready to go down to the hospital where she helped out with the volunteers' shop. She opened her dressing-table drawer to find her scarf and, as she was rummaging, found one of Jack's handkerchiefs. As she held it, a tidal wave of pain, of desolate loss, washed over her body. She was hardly able to breathe and began to sob.*

This is the point at which to accept that the feeling must be experienced and tolerated, at least for a while. There will probably be a chance to use distraction again later, in order to gain some respite. But for the moment, the individual needs to feel the desolation of loss. The same principle applies to all other crises.

The emotions, flashbacks and distressing thoughts are made more bearable by talking about them to someone else. This universal remedy for human ills is a very powerful one. We are fundamentally social animals, and when in distress there is great value in expressing our feelings to a sympathetic listener. In most crises there is a need to talk about it over and over again, in order to do the mental work necessary for the information to be assimilated. With each telling the feelings are re-experienced, so that they gradually become less frightening.

This particular issue has profound implications for professionals who work with people in crisis. Experienced workers in this field know that it is not giving advice or sharing activity that really counts, but the ability to stay with the person as they experience the most frightening and intense emotion. This means containing the emotion without trying to minimise it, talk the person out of it, or pretend it is not really so bad. Although it is basically a very simple thing, containing powerful emotion is not as easy as it sounds. In the next chapter, *Helping and being helped*, we shall consider why.

In what other ways can individuals make these powerful and painful feelings more bearable? A common and helpful approach is 'talking to oneself'. People tell themselves things all the time in any case, a running mental commentary on what is happening, how they are feeling. Usually this 'self-talk' is not attended to, it is beyond awareness, although people can learn to pay attention to it and are often surprised by what they discover. In crisis, when the emotional system is aroused, it is common for this self-talk to become more conscious, and for people to tell themselves things which will have a regulating effect on the problematic emotion. Anxiety can be regulated by reassuring or calming phrases; depression can be allayed by a conscious reminder of a positive side to the picture. It is as if a caring and reasoning part of the person were trying to calm a 'distressed child' part. Benign self-talk can be very useful in helping people ride out a peak of all-but-intolerable emotion without feeling completely overwhelmed and out of control. The stronger the feeling, the more conscious the effort to reason with oneself becomes, even to the point of speaking aloud or writing things down.

It is possible that this 'self-talk' is really more like an internal dialogue. On the one hand, as described in Chapter 2, powerful emotions trigger particular kinds of thoughts – automatic, negative or catastrophic. Here is a selection of the most common ones:

— 'I won't be able to get through this.'

— 'I'm going mad.'

— 'This is terrible: my life is ruined.'

— 'I'll never feel happy again.'

— 'No one can help me or understand how it feels.'

— 'Something even worse is going to happen.'

— 'I am completely alone.'

— 'There's no point in life if such horrible things can happen.'

— 'I'm sure I'm having a heart attack: it keeps missing beats.'

Just imagine for a moment that, as an experiment, you wanted to make yourself feel bad. How would you go about it? One very effective way would be to say these phrases over and over again in your mind. Better still, record them on a cassette tape and play it constantly over headphones as you try to concentrate on a task. This is more or less equivalent to what is happening in crisis. The powerful emotional reaction triggers this type of thinking automatically, even against the person's will. A conscious effort to tell oneself something different, to change the script, is therefore very useful as it breaks the vicious circle between thought and feeling. Here are some examples of the kinds of counter-statement commonly used by those effectively coping with powerful distress:

▶ 'I can come through this – just hang on.'

▶ 'I've been in difficult situations before and it turned out okay.'

▶ 'Nothing more awful is going to happen.'

▶ 'These feelings are horrible but they won't harm or damage me.'

▶ 'Just live each day as it comes; don't worry about the future.'

▶ 'This feeling won't last for ever – it will get better.'

▶ 'Other people have had worse things happen and have survived it.'

▶ 'I've got to go through this and see what good comes out of it.'

This type of self-talk aims to tackle the catastrophic thoughts directly. It is giving access to positive memories and beliefs about self and others. This releases internal resources in a situation which taxes the person's normal capacity to tolerate stress.

There are other things people say to themselves which provide self-guidance or internal resources, and it is worth examining three such strategies. All these require that the person is not in the throes of a very powerful emotion such as despair or panic. They are therefore 'second line' strategies, to be adopted when the most powerful feeling has already been contained to some degree. All three can be purely mental, but the impact may be enhanced by writing down one's thoughts.

Strategy 1. Think of someone you admire and value. Then imagine that this person has experienced exactly the same crisis as you. What would he or she feel in the same situation, and what would they do? Sometimes this exercise is difficult because one immediately thinks, 'Oh no, she would never get herself into this mess in the first place!' Even so, just imagine she did – what would she do then? The answers are often very helpful, either giving access to a new approach or reaffirming that one is doing everything that can be done and that there is no cause for self-reproach or worry.

Strategy 2. Consciously remind yourself that the emotional reaction is natural, only to be expected. During a crisis, almost everyone makes the mistake of taking the emotional turmoil too personally, as if it implied something bad about oneself. So, for example:

- I must be a weak, pathetic person to be crying so much.

- These flashbacks are going on too long. I'm sure there's something wrong with me.

- I can't think straight or concentrate on anything – I must be losing my mind.

People tend to be very tough on themselves. If a close friend or relative were suffering a similar crisis, one might be very understanding, explaining that such reactions are only to be expected. Yet with ourselves we are less forgiving, and make quite unrealistic internal demands to get on with life as if nothing had happened. Beneath this, there is sometimes a fear that other people will tire and become less sympathetic unless you 'pull yourself together'. It is sometimes a case of 'Don't be hard on me; I'm being hard enough on myself.' There is a realistic element to this fear, and how to judge what others can tolerate will be explored in the next chapter. In any case, nothing is to be gained by inferring personal weakness from the crisis reactions. An important coping method is consciously to remind oneself that such reactions are natural, normal and predictable. If the victim is unaware of this, there is value in the helpers giving them some straightforward information about the natural emotional sequel to crisis.

Strategy 3. Another way of gaining access to internal resources which are temporarily blocked is to draw up a list of the qualities one needs in the current situation. The list might include courage, fortitude and a sense of humour, for example. Then one consciously sets about remembering, in detail, past times when one showed those particular qualities. This process of dwelling on and entering into past situations makes it possible to realise that one is not defined by the sum total of one's present emotions (for example: at this moment I am frightened like a lost child) but that there are other aspects of oneself which can be made accessible. Think: when did you ever show courage? The mental search may bring to mind a situation which you then allow yourself to enter into as fully as possible. What did it feel like to be courageous? How did other people react? A similar mental search can bring into awareness the personal experiences of endurance, religious insight, a sense of humour, concern for others, problem-solving ability, facing difficulties as a challenge, taking an objective view of a confusing situation, and so on. Of course, these 'memories' are harder to reach when one is in the grip of the opposite emotion – hence the need for a conscious effort – but it can be done. The value of this method is the extent to which one can re-experience and focus attention on the internal cues of the positive resource, imaginatively and vividly re-entering the experience rather than just recalling it in the abstract.

COPING WITH THE PROBLEM

Whilst tolerating and assuaging the feelings, there is often a problem or a series of problems to be faced. Active forms of coping aim to change an aspect of the situation, to tackle a problem directly. We can include here changing one's own behaviour. Problem-focused coping methods will vary widely in their specific details because of the range of difficulties to be tackled, unlike emotion-focused coping, which, because the emotional responses to crisis are universal, can be described in general terms.

There are very few crises which do not allow for any constructive action.

❑ *A man whose 20-year-old son was killed in a car accident by a drunken driver imagined afterwards that his son would have said to him, 'Dad, don't let this happen to anyone else'. He began a successful campaign against drinking and driving, raising public awareness of the problem and providing a support network for those who had suffered similar losses.*

This might seem an extreme example, but it does demonstrate that people who have suffered appalling loss can and do find ways to alter the world as a result of their experience. Even though this father could do nothing to bring his son back, by his actions he gave the death – and his own life – a meaning and purpose.

The personal outcome of many crises can be altered by the active, problem-focused coping efforts we make. The problem is to know in advance how much scope we have to change things. There are no guarantees about this: the only certainty is that one cannot achieve something one has not attempted. Deciding what can be done involves making a judgement, and one is inevitably influenced both by current emotions and by previous experience.

Take someone who, before the crisis, has rarely had the experience of successfully acting upon the world to change things. In addition, depressed mood has produced a sense of hopelessness. Such a person is not likely even to contemplate active coping, even if there are many things which could be done to improve the situation.

❑ *'I'm really worried about you, Jan.' It was nearly six weeks since Pete walked out, and Janice Bowers's friend Lorraine had come to see her late one morning. She found her still in bed, and the house was in a mess. Lorraine felt quite angry. 'Are you going to let that little turd ruin your life? For God's sake get a grip!' Janice began to cry and said there was nothing she could do. Everyone knew what had happened and people were laughing about it. She hadn't any money and the kids were playing up terribly. Everything was hopeless. Her friend was unimpressed by this. 'Well have you seen the solicitor yet about maintenance? What about keeping yourself looking presentable and getting out and meeting people? There must be someone you know who could lend you some money. I'd be happy to look after the kids one evening.' Janice just sighed and shook her head.*

Janice just cannot believe that she has any power to change things. She has been brought up to think of herself as a victim of other people's actions rather than as an actor in her own right. She has not had many experiences of facing a challenge and succeeding. Even worse, real achievements (such as bringing up two young children) are not seen as 'work' and are not valued. The lack of belief in one's own efficacy is a major stumbling-block to problem solving, because one does not even attempt to change things. This attitude rarely alters overnight, but people in Janice's position can learn to take a more active stance towards their problems.

In contrast to the person who feels like this, someone who has acted effectively in the past, perhaps thinking of him- or herself as 'a fighter', is less likely to be overwhelmed by helpless feelings and will judge the possibility of constructive action more favourably. This is an important difference between people. Those who consistently respond to stressful events as if they are a challenge, and who see themselves as having a chance of changing things , are less likely to become ill as a result of crisis

VULNERABILITY TO CRISIS QUIZ

EXERCISE 5

Answer each question:
Y = Yes, I agree;   *P* = Perhaps, I'm not sure;   *N* = No, I disagree

		Y	P	N
1.	It's hardly worth working hard in your job since most times other people get the benefit of it.	__	__	__
2.	I like it when something unexpected happens to break up the routine of the working day.	__	__	__
3.	When someone in authority has made a decision there's nothing much you can do about it.	__	__	__
4.	I've found that most of my misfortunes have happened because of mistakes I've made.	__	__	__
5.	Life is an interesting adventure.	__	__	__
6.	It upsets me a great deal if other people get annoyed with me.	__	__	__
7.	If someone has it in for you there's not much point in trying to reason with them.	__	__	__
8.	Every problem has a solution.	__	__	__
9.	I often feel let down by people I thought I could trust.	__	__	__
10.	Most problems will go away if you ignore them.	__	__	__
11.	People can avoid problems by planning their lives.	__	__	__
12.	I think you can get most things you want if you try hard enough.	__	__	__
13.	I've found people are generally very ungrateful for things you do for them.	__	__	__
14.	You always have some freedom of choice even in difficult situations.	__	__	__
15.	I enjoy listening to other people and hearing about their experiences.	__	__	__

Score as follows:
Questions 2, 5, 8, 11, 12, 14, 15: Y=0, P=1, N=2
Questions 1, 3, 4, 6, 7, 9, 10, 13: Y=2, P=1, N=0

Below 5:	You are exceptionally resilient to crisis stress.
5 – 10:	You manage to face most crises successfully.
11 – 15:	You may find yourself knocked sideways by stress at times.
Above 15:	You are probably very vulnerable to the effects of crisis.

stress. At present, we just don't know whether this is because such people are able to take constructive action, with the consequence that their crises have less serious practical repercussions; or whether it is a purely psychological phenomenon, and some people are more 'immune' from the effects of stress. Perhaps it is a mixture of both. It does suggest that the victim's expectations will influence the outcome of the crisis.

At this point you should complete Exercise 5, which will give you some idea of whether you are vulnerable to crisis stress or relatively immune. Remember, though, that this is not an infallible method of measurement, and also that personal immunity is only one of many factors which act together to produce the eventual outcome.

An appraisal of what practical things are possible can help the individual to make a plan. As with emotion-focused coping, this can be a mental plan but is even more useful if written down. The plan will be a guide to action, laying out the possibilities, reminding one of the tasks ahead and the next step. At a time when normal mental processes are impaired, it is a valuable aid to concentration, memory and organisational ability. It also introduces an element of certainty and control into a bewildering situation, and this is probably a major (emotion-regulating) function. Whether the plan gives one real control or just the illusion of control is probably not really important – what matters is that the plan provides the *feeling* of having some control, of being able to regain some ability to predict the future. The professional worker can often help someone begin the process of deciding on a plan of action and act as a sounding-board for their ideas. The skill here is in standing back, not making the plan *for* the person but helping them to do it for themselves. There is more detail on the professional's role in the next chapter.

SEARCHING FOR INFORMATION

The first step towards changing something is to become better informed about the problem. Although the individual in crisis has entered personally uncharted territory, knowing little about what is happening and what is likely to happen, it is almost certain that other people have experienced a similar problem and can give the benefit of their knowledge. Advice might be sought from someone who has personally been in a similar situation, from a specialist source of expertise (either professional or voluntary), or from books.

Helen Smith, you remember, had an operation to remove the cancerous tumour from her breast. The rest of her breast was left intact and she was given radiotherapy.

❏ *Soon after she returned from hospital, Helen went to the local library and
borrowed all the books she could find about breast cancer and mastectomy. The
book she found most helpful was an autobiographical account of a woman who had
gone through a similar ordeal, in fact even worse since she had lost her whole
breast with very little warning. Helen happened to mention this book to a friend,
who said that her husband's cousin had had the same operation and would be
happy to talk to her about it. Helen phoned her the next day, and when they met
she found it very calming and helpful to hear someone talking easily about what
had happened six years before. She felt so relieved – the future now seemed a far
more real possibility.*

Here Helen has found out what other people would do or have done in
the same situation, both by meeting them and by reading books. This
basic strategy can be followed in almost every crisis. Like making a plan,
information gathering reduces uncertainty and gives a sense of control
as well as preparing the way for further action. What that action can be
depends ultimately on the circumstances.

SEEKING HELP

Let's look at two examples of a problem-focused approach.

❏ *The evening of the day he punched the consultant psychiatrist, Ben Martin sat
for an hour with his head in his hands, thinking. He kept remembering what had
happened, and each time it gave him a shudder. The irony was that he hated
violence of any kind. He felt humiliated and ashamed. He also felt exhausted, but
that was temporarily forgotten in his turmoil. Without thinking, he went to the
fridge to open another can of beer, but something made him stop. 'That's not going
to solve anything, you idiot – you're in a mess and you've got to sort it out.' Half
an hour later he had made a decision. He picked up the phone and dialled his friend
Mike. The words were hard to get out, even though he had rehearsed them. 'Hey
Mike, I've got a problem. Could you come round? I need someone to talk to.'*

*The next morning Ben got into work early. It took him two hours to clear up his
desk, putting files away and sorting things into separate piles. By the time Karen
arrived it was transformed. He told her what had happened and she was
surprisingly helpful. She offered to cover some of his day's work for him. Then Ben
made three phone calls. One was to his union rep. He arranged to see her at lunch-
time to find out about the likelihood of disciplinary proceedings and what would
happen then. The second was to one of the psychologists in the hospital who ran
workshops on 'managing job stress', asking if he could book for the next one. He'd
always made jokes about these in the past, but somehow it wasn't so funny now.
The final call was the hardest to make. He had to take a few deep breaths and his
hand was shaking. It was to his own manager. 'Oh hello John, it's Ben here. You'll
be getting a call from Dr Galloway this morning making a complaint about me.*

Can I come and see you about it as soon as possible?' Funnily enough, after making that call he felt much better. It wasn't as difficult as he thought it would be to draft the letter. 'Dear Dr Galloway, I am really very sorry about what happened yesterday . . .'

One thing strikes us immediately. For some people, like Ben, a crisis is a positive force in waking them up to the fact that they have a problem and that they need help. Ben has previously avoided solving his difficulties. He did not have any motive to change, perhaps because he felt that facing up to things was more unpleasant than the alternative. Now something has happened which has presented him with a vision of himself and his behaviour which is so discordant with his own aspirations that he feels anxious and ashamed. This shock has forced him to think seriously about what is happening. Of course, not everyone responds to a crisis in this way. It would have been possible for Ben to continue to run away from his problem, blaming his colleagues, the job, his workload – blaming anything and everything but not wanting to take responsibility himself. Ben's decision to take responsibility does not mean that his colleagues are always reasonable, that his job is easy or that his workload is fair. Making a decision to tackle a problem does not remove the need for action by others who may have contributed to the problem.

Ben has coped by getting help from other people to solve the problem, and this is generally a valuable strategy. He uses four people – one to provide him with personal support, one to give practical help, one to give him specialist help with his job stress, and one to give him information about the disciplinary procedures he will probably be facing. In most crises people need more than one kind of help, and the ability to mobilise it depends both on the individual and on the kind of social network to which they belong. Ways of finding and using help will be discussed in the next chapter.

Ben has also made a start on sorting out his workload problems, by the almost symbolic act of tidying his desk and by making an appointment to see his manager before he is summoned to do so. The latter act of 'grasping the nettle' is another active form of coping which can pay dividends when something unpleasant has to be faced. By taking the initiative in this way one is signalling to others a desire to be constructive, and this invites a constructive response. Of course, grasping the nettle needs some courage, and that implies going ahead even though one feels anxious. Without fear, there would be no courage.

LIFESTYLE CHANGES

Problem-focused coping is obviously valuable in Ben's situation, since many of the problems were partly of his own making and will clearly respond to his efforts. Is there a role for this active form of practical coping in crises which are out of our own control? The story of Paul Stanton, the young man facing AIDS, offers some answers to this question.

◻ *It turned out that Paul had pneumonia, for which he was treated in hospital. After he returned home, he felt much better for a while. His friends rallied round and he began to go to meetings of a group for AIDS sufferers. With Toby's support, he began to make some practical arrangements. He made a will and sorted out his finances. They knew that the top-floor flat would be an impossibly difficult place to live when Paul became weaker, and they found a ground-floor flat which had a small garden.*

Paul said to his closest friends, 'We're all going to die, but for me it's sooner not later. I'm going to make the most of the time I have – I'm looking for quality of life.' He gave up his job and started to follow those interests he had never had time to develop: cooking, gardening and reading. He had always wanted a dog, so he and Toby chose a West Highland puppy. He began to take an interest in what he ate. He started to take daily exercise, walking with the puppy on Hampstead Heath. One spring morning he was out there as the sun was rising. As he sat and looked at the little Westie shuttling backwards and forwards, suddenly it all seemed so beautiful – it was wonderful to be alive. And yet, paradoxically, at that precise moment and for the first time, it seemed all right to die.

Paul has used a wide range of emotionally orientated coping strategies – suppression and distraction alternating with fully experiencing the feelings and talking about them. He has also consciously begun to re-evaluate the meaning of his life in the light of his imminent death. He has sought help from others. He has started to tackle some important practical problems that the future holds both for himself and the man he loves. Finally, he has paid attention to taking care of himself in order to stay as well as possible for as long as possible. Thus problem-focused coping is indeed of value to many people facing the uncontrollable, who can take very active steps to gain the best quality of life possible. This 'fighting spirit' also allows a recognition of when it is appropriate to re-linquish striving and attempting to retain control, when it is enough just to *be*, in the way Paul discovered on the Heath one morning.

Coping by *taking care of oneself* is generally helpful during crisis. Actively striving to increase well-being is a practical task often over-looked, as people tend to neglect themselves whilst emotionally pre-occupied. It is very easy when depressed or anxious to skip meals, to eat convenience or junk food very quickly, to drink far too much alcohol, tea and coffee but not enough plain water, to avoid baths and showers, fresh air and exercise. When working with a person in crisis, it is worth check-ing out with them whether they are neglecting self-care. People often need someone from outside, someone whose opinion carries weight with them, to give guidance on diet and exercise and to suggest concrete and simple ways in which they could stop self-neglect. In Chapter 6, *Managing stress*, a number of specific ways of taking care will be explored.

REGAINING CONFIDENCE

Problem-focused coping may include following a plan to regain confidence after the crisis. For example, many people who have been in a car accident or train crash are frightened to drive or to travel on a train. Giving in to this fear by avoiding that form of travel is likely to lead to long-term problems, since avoiding the source of fear is like pouring petrol on a fire: the anxiety is likely to get worse over time, not better, and may generalise to other travel situations. From the discussion in the last chapter, we can see why this might be. The belief that has been confronted by the accident is 'I am living in a safe world'. The task ahead is to come to terms with the reality that the world is not as safe as one thought, *and that it never was*. But this does not stop people living ordinary lives or travelling in cars and trains. The only way to learn this is to expose oneself to the feared situation. The alternative, avoidance, is like saying 'The world will continue to be perfectly safe as long as I don't go on trains'. But of course this isn't true – there is always some risk, always some potential for danger. Anxiety thrives on this potential, because the fear that something might happen next time is never tested against reality. Thus it is possible to become frightened of travelling alone, then of travelling at all, then of leaving the house, and so on.

An active way to tackle this problem is to go back, to repeat the experience of travelling. This can be done with a friend or relative, someone who can tolerate one's distress and stay with it. If the ordeal of repeating the journey seems unmanageable, it can be built up gradually, in stages: for example, by just getting into the car first, then going for a short trip, then a longer one, and so on. During this procedure, using some method to manage one's anxiety can be very valuable. (Methods for controlling anxiety will be described in Chapter 6.)

Having thought about the range of coping strategies people use to handle crisis, you might like to explore your own coping style. Exercise 6 gives you a chance to do this.

YOUR COPING STYLE

EXERCISE 6

Return to your notes on Exercises 2 and 3. Which of the following statements best describes your own response to that crisis? Score each item in the following way:

1 = Not at all.
2 = To some extent.
3 = Yes, I did this.
4 = Yes, very much so.

Score

1. Took things one step at a time and worked out what to do next. ☐
2. Stopped myself worrying too much over things I couldn't control. ☐
3. Got professional help. ☐
4. Wished I could change what had already happened. ☐
5. Worked harder to sort things out. ☐
6. Took to the bottle (either alcohol or pills). ☐
7. Made a plan of action and kept to it. ☐
8. Daydreamed, imagining a better situation than the one I was in. ☐
9. Accepted sympathy and understanding from someone. ☐
10. Went to bed and slept a lot. ☐
11. Accepted that my feelings were natural in the situation. ☐
12. Hoped for a miracle to happen to make things come out right. ☐
13. Kept calming myself down and telling myself I would come through. ☐
14. Tried to prevent other people seeing how I felt. ☐
15. Talked to someone about the situation. ☐

How do you score?

Add up your score separately for the following items?
1, 5, 7: Coping with the problem.
4, 8, 12: Wishful thinking.
3, 9, 15: Seeking support.
6, 10, 14: Avoidance.
2, 11, 13: Coping with feelings.

Where do you score highest and lowest? From this you will be able to see your *coping style* in this situation. If you score high on wishful thinking and avoidance compared to coping with feelings, coping with the problem and seeking support, you may have difficulties following a crisis. Chapter 4 might help you appraise your coping style and think about different ways of reacting in future.

Chapter Five

Helping And Being Helped

Have you noticed how much our society values independence and personal achievement? Everyone seems to be striving to get on in life and we admire those who are strong, who can cope on their own, who don't seem to need anyone else. It is easy to forget that total independence is something of an illusion. In fact we live in a web of interconnections, from the food we eat and the clothes we wear to our need for human companionship. Every one of us lives in a social network of mutual interdependence. Until quite recently, people lived within one group of kin and neighbours, say about fifty people. Now relationships are made and broken more readily, with greater geographical and social mobility. We are no longer guaranteed a lifetime's social network. In modern life, the concept of 'duty' to family and friends is not so widespread. Despite this, both routinely and in a crisis, people have a need for a system of mutual aid and to belong to a social group.

Linked to these social changes is the emergence of the caring professions, who are skilled in the relatively modern practice of helping strangers. Trained specialists are engaged in helping people who are sick, elderly, destitute, who have psychiatric or learning difficulties or who experience problems at work, in marriage or with child care. Even so, most help is still provided within families or between friends, and this applies in crisis as much as or more than in routine circumstances.

THE SOCIAL NETWORK – A NATURAL HELP SYSTEM

The social network provides natural channels for help to become available to people in crisis. Understanding social networks is a vital part of effective helping in crisis because skilled helping should enhance the mobilisation of support from within the person's own natural social system. Unfortunately, without realising it, professionals can sometimes work against the natural support system, preventing rather than encouraging the mobilisation of help from family and friends. The professional's role in crisis help is to supplement natural resources where they are not adequate and to facilitate them where there is a problem with support mobilisation. For both these tasks, a working knowledge of how help becomes available within social networks is very useful.

A good way of understanding networks in general is to start by understanding one's own, and an exercise is given later to help you do this. Having mapped out one's own network it is easy to show someone else how it is done. But first, here are some basic principles.

A network consists of the people one knows to meet and talk to regularly, plus those other significant people from whom one is geographically separated but who would be available if you needed them. Networks have a size and a structure, and this is important in understanding normal patterns of crisis help. Size is an obvious feature. Large networks tend to be heterogeneous, containing people from different backgrounds. If one knows many different types of people it is likely that there will be more than one kind of help available. Assuming a certain size of network, the structure and strength of ties is just as important. Knowing many people on the level of acquaintanceship but with no intimates may provide plenty of practical help and information but is less helpful for emotional expression and companionship.

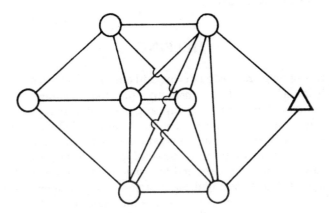

Figure 5.1: Small, dense kinship network (N=8, D=64.3%)

Another influence on the availability of help is whether or not the network is closely knit. Where many network members know each other, perhaps through kinship (technically this is called a high-density network: see Figure 5.1), crisis help can be mobilised very quickly. This is simply because only one person in the network needs to know about the crisis in order to bring about discussion among other network members. In this way people 'rally round': for example, giving the person a lift, cooking meals, organising a funeral, going through legal papers, looking after children, and so on. In a loose-knit system this is much more difficult, because individuals will not know each other and the person in crisis has to make more effort to inform everyone about what is happening. The speed of communication is reduced. Later on, there may be disadvantages to a small dense network, since it is more difficult to develop new roles or a new identity when everyone you know knows one another. In a tight network, it is possible to become 'locked into' an old identity. For example, a woman who is widowed will at some stage need to move on from being 'John's wife' to developing new facets of herself. This is easier if there is a loosely knit network which offers social circumstances where she can experiment with a new identity. The same is true of any identity transition.

Perhaps the ideal network is one which combines the virtues of belonging to a closely knit group with those of having available a wide range of information and skills. This is a large network with dense subclusters within it, as illustrated in Figure 5.2. What kind of network do you inhabit? Where would your help come from in a crisis? If you would like to find out, complete Exercise 7. This shows you how to draw a picture of your network and to see where different kinds of help are potentially available.

HELPING

What forms of help are needed during and after a crisis? What is the best way of helping? I shall discuss helping under four headings: emotional support, information, companionship, and practical help. As we examine each one in detail, we shall see how these kinds of help are intimately linked with the types of coping method discussed in the last chapter. In fact one of the main purposes of crisis support is to facilitate the individual's own coping responses and to promote a wider range of coping. This is consistent with seeing those in crisis as active responders, so that help is not just doing things *for* them (which can diminish people and produce dependency) but *with* them (which promotes self-efficacy). We shall return to the difference between enabling and disabling help later.

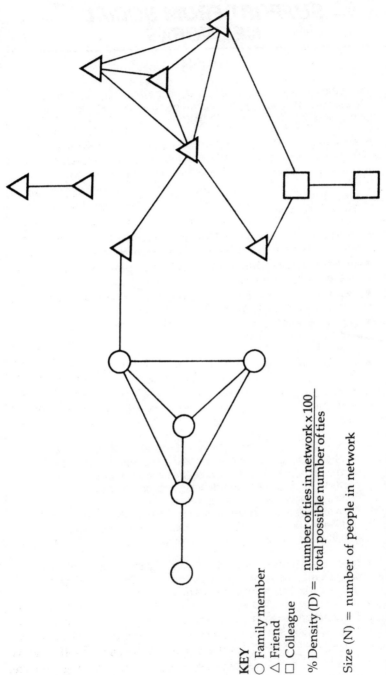

KEY

○ Family member
△ Friend
□ Colleague

% Density (D) = $\dfrac{\text{number of ties in network} \times 100}{\text{total possible number of ties}}$

Size (N) = number of people in network

Figure 5.2: Low density social network (N=15, D=20%)

SUPPORT FROM SOCIAL NETWORKS

EXERCISE 7

This Exercise takes quite a time, but most people find the results interesting and, what is more, you will be able to use the technique with your clients if you have first practised it on yourself.

▶ First, make a list of people in your social network in the spaces on the left of the grid on pages 66 & 67. (There is room for 20 people; if you want to include more, add more spaces.) How do you decide who to include and who to leave out? The following guidelines will lead to a workable network for understanding crisis support. Write down the names of:

- *Members of your family* whom you see regularly. (Exclude distant relations you never see or see only at formal family gatherings.)
- *Friends* you see regularly or with whom you keep in contact by letter and telephone.
- *Neighbours,* if you regularly go into each other's homes. (Exclude neighbours with whom you pass the time of day in the street.)
- *Colleagues,* if you have frequent contact and feel there is a personal relationship (but exclude those with whom you have only formal, impersonal contact).
- *Include* anyone else who is emotionally significant to you, although you may be temporarily estranged or separated.
- *Exclude* casual acquaintances, purely professional contacts (eg dentist, accountant) or people you know only through someone else.

▶ After making the list, start with name 1 and go along the row; the numbers along the top refer to the other people on the list. Under each column, ask 'Do these two people have a relationship with each other?' If in doubt about defining 'relationship', use the same criteria as above. Place a tick in each box where a relationship definitely exists, and a question mark if there is only a weak relationship or if you are not sure. Repeat this procedure for Name 2, Name 3 and so on until the grid is complete.

▶ Next, for each person, tick (using the four right-hand columns) if you would turn to this person for support in a crisis. The kind of support you would look to them for is as follows:

E = emotional support
P = practical help
C = companionship
A = advice and information

▶ Then take a plain piece of paper and sketch out a diagram of your network using circles to represent relatives, triangles for friends and squares for colleagues (see Fig 5.2 for an example). Draw a solid line between two people who have a tick, and a dotted line for a question mark. You may need two or three sketches before you are happy with the best way of arranging the people and the lines between them.

▶ Take four copies of the final diagram and take four different coloured pens to represent the four types of support. On each diagram separately, highlight your potential sources of support. (You can do this all on the one diagram, but it might become muddled and hard to see the different colours clearly.)

Analysing the social network and support diagram

You now have a social network diagram which highlights the sources of four different types of help. The following questions will help you think about the results:

? How many people are there in your network? (An average size would be about 12, but remember that quality is just as important as quantity.)

? Is your network high or low density? (That is, are there many lines between all the members or only a few?)

? Are there sub-clusters of relatively dense groups linked only by one or two solid or dotted lines?

? Is your network dominated by one group, whether relatives, friends or colleagues or does it contain people from all these domains?

Now look at the four types of social support. Are you using the whole of your network for support or only a small proportion of it? Are the same few people being used for all four types of support or do you spread the load? Is there any one type of support which is clearly lacking in your network?

Thinking about these questions will often reveal ways in which you are not mobilising help as effectively as you could. As you read the rest of this chapter, you will come to understand why.

NAME	1	2	3	4	5	6	7	8	9	
1	★									
2	★	★								
3	★	★	★							
4	★	★	★	★						
5	★	★	★	★	★					
6	★	★	★	★	★	★				
7	★	★	★	★	★	★	★			
8	★	★	★	★	★	★	★	★		
9	★	★	★	★	★	★	★	★	★	
10	★	★	★	★	★	★	★	★	★	
11	★	★	★	★	★	★	★	★	★	
12	★	★	★	★	★	★	★	★	★	
13	★	★	★	★	★	★	★	★	★	
14	★	★	★	★	★	★	★	★	★	
15	★	★	★	★	★	★	★	★	★	
16	★	★	★	★	★	★	★	★	★	
17	★	★	★	★	★	★	★	★	★	
18	★	★	★	★	★	★	★	★	★	
19	★	★	★	★	★	★	★	★	★	
20	★	★	★	★	★	★	★	★	★	

WORK GRID

	12	13	14	15	16	17	18	19	20	E	P	C	A
	★												
	★	★											
	★	★	★										
	★	★	★	★									
	★	★	★	★	★								
	★	★	★	★	★	★							
	★	★	★	★	★	★	★						
	★	★	★	★	★	★	★	★					
	★	★	★	★	★	★	★	★	★				

ASSESSING WHAT HELP YOU SHOULD GIVE

Before any type of helping is undertaken, judgements need to be made about what the person needs and what you are realistically able to offer. What the person needs is not necessarily the same as what he or she wants. What you are able to give may fall short of what is being asked of you. Many inexperienced helpers rush in with the best of intentions without making any appraisal of these things. They try to respond generously to what the person seems to want, but sometimes things end badly.

❑ *A young hospital chaplain was ministering to a woman who was in the last stages of a final illness. At the bedside he often saw her daughter, who visited daily. After her mother's death he offered her the opportunity to talk things over. She began to see him from time to time, felt she could trust him, and confided in him fully about her loneliness and her feelings about losing her mother, who had been the most important person in her life. He responded warmly and compassionately, saying she could come and see him 'anytime' and gave her his home telephone number. They sometimes met for coffee in town. He visited her home during the day on several occasions. Sometimes their talks were quite intimate, and on one occasion he talked about his own experience of loss.*

After six months, there was no sign of her needing to phone him or see him less frequently. Indeed on one occasion she clearly did not want him to leave and began to cry when he insisted. He began to worry that she was becoming too dependent on him and suggested less frequent meetings. On one occasion when she phoned him he said he would call her back but forgot to do so for several weeks. When he did phone, she seemed subdued and quite cold and did not ask to see him. Feeling sad, but also quite relieved, he did not contact her again. Two weeks later he had a note from her: 'You said you were my friend, and I believed you. Now I know not to trust anyone again.' The note caused him a good deal of pain, but he reminded himself of how much time he had given her during the crisis of her acute grief, and felt she had unreasonable expectations. He decided it would be wrong to get drawn in a second time. He wrote a brief note saying he was sorry she felt that way, that he was still her friend, and perhaps she would come to see things differently in time. He did not suggest meeting. A week later he heard from a colleague that she was a patient in the psychiatric wing. She had taken a serious overdose and was still feeling suicidal.

What has gone wrong here? For a start, the chaplain has not stood back and decided what he is able to give and what he cannot give. It might sound very cold and calculating to talk in this way. Surely altruism is by definition not concerned with this kind of calculation? Perhaps, but it is really a matter of being honest about one's motives and not misleading people by offering more than one can give. There has been a fundamental misunderstanding, in this example, between the helper and the person he was trying to help. In her needy state, the bereaved and unhappy woman felt she had at last found someone who could be trusted always to be there and never to abandon her. The chaplain was trying to offer solace and human companionship to help her through the acute stage of her grief, and probably deep down expected her to be grateful and reasonable. He could not see the dangers of his apparent offer of friendship. Getting out of one's depth does not help the crisis-stricken person, and can make things worse.

A metaphor might be useful here. Imagine you see someone fall through thin ice in the middle of a frozen pond. You can see she is in deep water and in distress. You are of no use to her if you stay on the bank waving and shouting advice, but nor is it helpful to rush into the middle of the pond and fall in with her. You keep one foot on the bank, and with the other foot you go out *as far as you safely can,* then you reach out. Helping is rather like this – a matter of keeping one foot on safe ground and reaching out.

The chaplain has learned something from his experience. He can see now that it would have been much more helpful to the bereaved woman in the long run if he had set clear boundaries around their talks *at the beginning.* A boundary defines a safe place for both parties, gives consistency, and helps to develop trust. Boundaries can be established in time, in space and in intimacy. For example, our chaplain could have suggested meeting once or twice a week for an hour. He could have consistently seen the bereaved woman in his own office. In not setting any boundaries, he was misleading her, promising an intimacy and friendship which, in reality, he was not offering. One of the commonest reasons for this kind of muddle is that we are unclear about our own motives for helping.

Why is it important to be aware of this? Sometimes our enthusiasm to help others is based on motives which are far from altruistic. Perhaps we help others because it makes us feel good about ourselves, because it gives us the rosy glow of moral virtue. Perhaps we help others because we want the reward of their gratitude and admiration. Sometimes we help because as children our role in the family was as 'helper', perhaps to a parent who was depressed or otherwise unable to meet our needs properly. In a case like this, helping others can continue into adult life as a way of covering up our own neediness and our resentment about not being cared for. Don't worry if you recognise yourself in one of these descriptions – they are all very common and natural reasons for people to be helpful to others, and do not in themselves detract from the value of the help given. The danger comes when we *blindly* use the person in crisis to meet one of our own unmet needs. This can trick us into behaving unwisely, perhaps by offering more than we can realistically give.

There are quite important and appropriate differences between the kinds of help offered by professional workers and those offered within the natural support system. In the following discussion I shall examine the whole range of help, including that given by friends and family.

EMOTIONAL SUPPORT

STAYING WITH THE FEELINGS

One thing should be clear enough by now. Crisis requires us to undergo emotional turmoil, and an important part of working through crisis is to find the capacity to bear psychological pain. The first, and in many ways most important, kind of help is simply to be with the person and provide a safe environment for them to experience it. Although I say 'simply be with the person', perhaps it is not as easy as it sounds.

This 'staying with' can be the most difficult thing to do, because the emotion of the crisis sufferer arouses very intense emotions in the helper too. It is a natural response to try and stop the person feeling their emotions, by cheering them up, talking them out of it, changing the subject, trying to distract them. It is not true that this is always unhelpful, since the individual wants and needs to avoid being overwhelmed by feelings so as to gain time, an opportunity to deal with the immediate problem in an active way. But at the point when the person in crisis is clearly ready and able to experience their feelings, it is extremely unhelpful. This is because the would-be helper is trying to avoid the emotions for the wrong reasons – because he or she finds them too upsetting.

Although it is helpful for the person in distress to be able to express their grief, fear, despair, shame or anger freely, in many ordinary networks this is the type of help which is most difficult to find. People often mistake the numb phase of suppression and distraction as evidence of a good recovery. They imagine that this shows how well the person is coping. When, later, there are outbursts of weeping, shaking, panic or horrifying flashbacks, family and friends are dismayed and might think that the person is 'breaking down'. Perhaps it is a relatively unusual person who is able to see someone they care for in extreme distress without either making a catastrophe of it or bustling round with paper tissues and cups of tea. These responses give a clear message: 'Please don't feel so distressed, *because I can't bear it.*' Skilled helping is a matter of being able to bear it. There is enormous value in being able to get in touch with the most deeply distressing feelings *and* contain them. This gives the message 'I can feel something of how painful and frightening this is. I can feel that you are afraid you will not be able to bear it. But I can take it – this feeling will not destroy either of us.'

The basic principle of being able to get in touch with powerful emotion in others without being knocked off balance yourself also applies when working with an angry person. As described in Chapter 2, *containing* angry emotions is different from and more effective than either appeasing or retaliating. The most common difficulty is that, faced with anger, we tend either to become frightened and intimidated or else we too feel angry. We become so caught up in our own emotional reactions that we stop seeing clearly how best to help the person. Some very basic guidelines for working in an angry crisis are shown in Box 5.1.

Box 5.1 Coping with anger in a crisis

- Keep reminding yourself not to take it personally – just because someone is angry with you does not mean you are a bad person!

- If there is any risk of attack, protect yourself from physical danger. (See *Facing Physical Violence*, in this series, for more guidance on this.)

- Consciously relax your muscles; and breathe deeply, not shallowly. (See Chapter 6 and *Managing Stress*, in this series, for guidance on relaxation.)

- Don't try to justify yourself.

- Don't argue back.

- Acknowledge that the person is feeling angry.

- Respond to *what* the person is saying rather than *how* they are saying it – try to understand the basic grievance.

- State your understanding of the grievance – don't try to get across your own point of view.

- Don't raise your voice. Speak as normally as possible and be prepared to drop your gaze – don't try to stare someone out.

- Don't try to resolve the problem there and then. Your aim is simply to contain the situation and prevent escalation.

HOW TO GIVE EMOTIONAL HELP

In listening carefully to what the person is saying and trying to understand what they are feeling, following some basic ground-rules will make it more helpful. Try to take your lead from the person rather than imposing your own ideas. This means reflecting back to them your understanding of what they are feeling rather than asking a lot of questions, giving advice or jumping to conclusions on the basis of what *you* would feel. By doing this you are unobtrusively acting as a mirror, a comforter and a container; giving back to the person a feeling of being heard and responded to, and giving them strong evidence that the feelings are not so overwhelming or dangerous as they feared.

Why is this form of 'being with' so valuable? Apart from making the emotions more bearable, it performs another vital role. Remember from the discussion in Chapter 3 that the person in crisis has had his or her fundamental sense of self challenged and disrupted. We all depend on others to some degree to maintain and regulate our theories about ourselves, the internal picture of 'me' and the feeling of being 'I'. Now the crisis has produced a deep confusion about that self. Emotional support of the kind we are discussing gives the individual a powerful experience of being attended to and responded to *as if he or she is a person of value who is known, recognised and cared for as an individual*. This is a way of giving coherence and validity to the self at a time when it is weakened and confused. Learning how to pay attention to people so that they feel understood is a skill which can be learned. (Some further reading on counselling skills is included in the bibliography.)

In Exercise 8 are some examples of alternative responses that a helper could make to people in the throes of powerful emotions during crisis. Try and pick the response which you think would be most likely to offer emotional support. (At the end of the book I have indicated which ones I would favour as the most supportive, but remember that these are not necessarily the only 'right' answers.)

PHYSICAL CONTACT

Emotional help within an intimate relationship is often physically nurturing. Comforting someone physically can include holding, stroking, rocking or massage. Physical comfort and affection provides some of the containment and mirroring mentioned above, with a component of regression to a time when as babies we were held and stroked and rocked. This can evoke profoundly comforting memories. Sometimes, though, a particular individual will shun all forms of physical comfort. This may be because, instead of evoking calm and nurtured feelings,

HELPFUL LISTENING

EXERCISE 8

This is not a test but a way to think about what is a helpful response to a person facing a crisis. Imagine someone has come to you for personal help. Each statement is followed by three possible responses that you might make. Which do you prefer? Do not be concerned if the wording of the response is not as you would phrase it; try to choose the type of answer you think best. My notes on the answers are on page 114.

1. Woman, age 32. Library assistant. Tense.

I just don't know what to do. I hate working for this boss; he's really got it in for me ever since I refused to go to his house for drinks one evening. He gets at me all the time now, picking at every little thing I do wrong. He humiliates me by criticising me in front of the others but I can't explain to anyone what's happening. I want to leave but he would give me a bad reference and I don't know if I'd get another job.

(a) This happens to lots of women if they don't give in to sexual harrassment. You were perfectly entitled not to go to his house so why should you be the one to pay for it? Let's think what you could do to get back at him and show him you can't be bullied.

(b) It's a difficult decision. I should think you feel pretty hurt he's picking on you. I guess you're feeling alone with it all.

(c) Let's think about that carefully. What are the pros and cons of leaving? Tell me more about the situation at work. It's possible you've got this whole thing out of proportion – it may not be as bad as it seems.

2. Man, age 37. Breathless.

I think I'm cracking up, I'm going to be a mental case. I can't sleep, I can't concentrate on anything. This problem at work has really got me down. Last night my heart was pounding and missing beats; I couldn't breathe properly; I had to get up and walk about. The doctor says there's nothing wrong with my heart but perhaps he's made a mistake – or perhaps I'm just imagining it. You'll think this is stupid but I really think I'm going crazy.

(a) Of course you're not going mad – you're just suffering anxiety symptoms, believe me. What's more, you can learn to control them you know; you don't have to feel that way.

(b) These symptoms are frightening and you're not feeling like your normal self. I should think you might feel you're losing control of things.

(c) I'm sure if the doctor says there's nothing wrong with your heart, then you'll be OK. You should take some time off, get a complete break, have a rest and probably in a week or two's time you'll feel a lot better.

3. Man. Mid-50's. Recently made redundant.

I haven't told my wife yet. I just leave the house at the same time every morning and drive to town and hang around the library. Sometimes I go for a long walk. I know she'll be so upset when she hears; I hope I can get something sorted out before I have to tell her.

(a) The thought of telling her is very upsetting. Perhaps if she knew, it would make it seem more real, and while she doesn't, it's like it hasn't really happened.

(b) I wonder if you're being fair to your wife? It will only cause her more pain when she does discover the truth, and she might be very hurt you don't trust her with this.

(c) You are denying the truth of what has happened because you find it just too painful and humiliating to face up to. But you can't run away for ever.

4. Man, age 26. Motorbike accident victim. Angry.

I can't walk and they say I might never be able to walk. There's not much point in living without any bloody legs. I wish I'd died in the crash not living on as a bloody cripple. I'd like to finish the job if I could.

(a) You're feeling very down right now and that's normal, but lots of people have severe physical disabilities and are still able to lead interesting and fulfilling lives.

(b) This sounds like self-pity to me. Who knows what the future holds? Isn't it selfish of you to be thinking of suicide after everyone has cared for you and your family have had such an ordeal?

(c) You're angry and feeling despair. It's a terrible loss, not to be able to walk, to run. It feels so hopeless and unfair you hardly know how to bear it.

5. Woman, 28. Weeping.

I loved that little baby, she was everything to me. When I found her, lying there . . . Oh God . . . it's just a nightmare, I just can't believe it. She was so small, so helpless. Why did she have to die?

(a) I don't know what to say. We just don't know why these things happen. It certainly wasn't your fault.

(b) Be strong, don't let yourself fall apart. Remember, you've got another child and a husband too. They need you now more than ever.

(c) It hurts, it hurts so much. (*pause*) You loved her so much and now she's gone.

6. Woman, age 20. Shuddering, shaking.

It was horrible, horrible. He just grabbed me and pushed me to the floor. Oh, God, I feel sick just thinking about it. He forced me to have sex with him and I just had to go along with it. I was so frightened.

(a) When did this happen? How did you get away? Have you been to the police yet?

(b) The bastard! Men who do that are really sick. God it must have been terrifying. I would be feeling just the same as you – really angry.

(c) It's like a nightmare for you. You've had a massive shock and I can see you're shaking with disgust and fear. He's hurt you.

it brings back frightening feelings of being vulnerable and out of control. The sensitive friend can read the signs and respond appropriately, not trying to impose physical comfort because of his or her own needs.

Professional workers are often muddled about if and when to offer physical comfort. In those moments of intense trauma when words cannot convey much, taking hold of someone's hand or putting an arm around his or her shoulders is simply a way of communicating your presence. On the other hand, there are definite problems with touching people you are working with professionally. Precisely because of its powerful regressive component, physical touch can blur the boundary between a realistic relationship and a fantasy one. This applies to both people in the encounter. It is hard to be clear about one's own motives for physical contact. Often the helper is trying to avoid his or her own fear that he or she has nothing much to offer, that 'just listening' is not much good because – you guessed it – the feelings are unbearable. In this way, the physical contact becomes a collusion with the fantasy that no one has the capacity to bear the emotional burden. The other problem is that the professional worker can be usurping the role of a spouse, a relative or a friend. The principle of facilitating natural forms of crisis support would suggest that physical comfort should be appropriately sought from the natural social network. But what if the person you are helping has a small, impoverished network where physical comfort is not easily available? Ironically, this would be an even stronger reason *not* to take on this function. The professional helper can fill a vacuum in the person's network, and by doing so make the individual less able to set about the task of finding new social resources. With the best of intentions, like our hospital chaplain, you could be absorbed into the problem rather than enabling someone to cope effectively.

GIVING INFORMATION AND ADVICE

Helping someone in a crisis by offering advice, guidance or information can facilitate active, problem-focused coping. These three types of help are related, differing in how disinterested (note: not *un*interested) the helper is. For example, compare these statements made to someone in a bereavement crisis:

- 'It's perfectly normal to be feeling like this now. It takes much longer than people imagine to come through grief.'

- 'If I were you I'd join the local CRUSE group. They really understand what you are going through.'

- 'You should get out more – it's not helping you being stuck in the house all the time. Next Saturday I am taking you to the pictures, and I won't take no for an answer.'

The first gives information, but holds no implications about what the helper wants the person to do. The second is guidance, clearly recommending a particular option. The third form of advice is even more directive. In general, non-directive information-giving is more appropriate to a professional relationship with the person in crisis. Directive advice is usually not in short supply from the individual's own network, whereas neutral, non-directive information may be.

Information is a valuable kind of help. The main difficulty for the helper is knowing when to give information or advice and when not to. The snag with this form of support is that people in crisis sometimes *seem* to be asking for advice when they are not ready to use it and are really expressing how they are feeling. A question like 'Oh please help me – what do you think I should do?' is usually a communication about how desperate or overwhelmed the person feels rather than a request for information. In this situation, the helper might respond with advice: for example, 'Well why don't you phone your solicitor?' or 'Have you heard about the organisation for people who have the same problem?' Helpers become disappointed or even annoyed when their good advice is brushed aside, or accepted half-heartedly but not acted upon. Timing is crucial. There will be a time when the person you are trying to help can use this type of guidance, but not while they are overwhelmed and preoccupied by their feelings. If any guidance is given, information about coping with powerful feelings would be more useful. Better still, start with the emotional support discussed earlier.

Some forms of professional counselling and psychotherapy explicitly avoid giving any advice or direct guidance. They focus entirely on helping clients to contain and clarify their feelings. The rationale is that this enables them to think things through for themselves and to find their own solutions. Practitioners of these methods know how easily advice-giving can interfere with the process of providing skilled emotional support.

Many who work with those in crisis, in both the professional and voluntary sectors, will not find it possible or even appropriate to take this 'pure' approach. Often one's role directly involves giving advice. Even so, making a careful judgement of how to time this and how to combine it with emotional help is very important and can save a great deal of time.

❑ *A young single mother came to see her health visitor in great distress. Her baby of fifteen months was not sleeping at night, and screaming if she did not go in and pick him up. The mother was at her wits' end. She asked for advice about how to solve the problem. The health visitor found that the mother was unwittingly rewarding the toddler for this behaviour with cuddles and games, and by taking him into her own bed and allowing him to sleep during the day. The problem was being maintained by these patterns, and there was a great deal that the mother could do to change things by using a systematic programme which the health visitor was happy to help her plan. Whilst explaining this, the health visitor began to feel more and more frustrated. Every suggestion she made seemed to be pushed aside. The mother seemed to invent one excuse after another for thinking her ideas impracticable. At the end of the meeting, the mother went away saying she would try some of these ideas. The health visitor was unconvinced, and felt a twinge of annoyance that the mother had been wasting her time.*

In this particular crisis, the mother is ostensibly asking for advice about solving her problem with the baby. She is exhausted, demoralised and possibly depressed. Her capacity to make decisions, to concentrate and to solve problems is reduced. She feels trapped, and may be frightened by her own violent impulses towards her child at moments of extreme stress. Perhaps, less consciously, she feels angry and victimised at being put in this position, feeling 'someone' should do something about it. Of course, there is absolutely nothing wrong with the health visitor's advice in itself. If this mother were ready and able to collaborate in a systematic programme, it would certainly be extremely helpful. But the mother does not want advice, because she has not yet reached the point of taking a problem-solving approach in her coping. From the information in the previous chapter, we can make a guess at what kind of coping she is using – possibly wishful thinking ('If I go to see the health visitor she'll sort it out for me') or avoidance ('I'll try not to think about it too much; perhaps it will sort itself out'). These are emotion-focused strategies, but not very effective ones. More effective emotional coping could be facilitated by helping the mother to express her feelings, and allowing her the experience of having them accepted and contained. When the emotions are contained, the person's capacity to think straight is enhanced and a problem-solving approach becomes possible. The health visitor would have found it more productive to spend quite some time *listening* to the mother and responding to her feelings. She might well have been able to establish a rapport; that is, the mother might have started to feel that someone understood her predicament. The central aim for the first talk should have been to give this feeling of being understood. In addition, it would have been helpful to bring the mother to the point of recognising for herself that she was utterly exhausted, that she was therefore not able to think clearly about things, and that the first priority was to enlist support from her own network so that she could have at least two consecutive nights' sleep.

Despite the problems of timing, I should not wish to give the impression that professional carers or managers should steer clear of giving advice and information. Professional workers are, by virtue of their training and experience, an excellent information resource for the community. They are generally a safe source of accurate information by virtue of their adherence to ethical codes and their acknowledgement of the limits of their competence. However, the role of the professions is limited, especially where advice is concerned. Any given professional is by definition a specialist, with in-depth knowledge about a specific aspect of a problem. It is inevitable that if someone in crisis consults us we tend to see the problem from our own point of view – the doctor will see it as a medical problem, the social worker as a social problem, the psychologist as a psychological problem, the teacher as an educational problem, and so on. There are many occasions when the individual needs a range of different kinds of information, and not necessarily of a kind which professionals can give. Other sources of information, such as voluntary advice centres, self-help groups or other people within the person's existing network, are often of equal value.

Getting information via one's own network depends on access to the right person with the right knowledge. This tends to be easier in large, low-density, heterogeneous networks. A valuable way to make a small network effectively much bigger is through a bridging tie. This is when someone in one's own network knows someone in a completely separate network. These bridging ties give access to a much wider range of information, and the same applies to practical help. Helen Smith is a good illustration of this. In her search for information about breast cancer and mastectomy, she used a bridging tie to very good effect.

☐ *Helen spoke to a friend who said that her husband's cousin had had the same operation and would be happy to talk to her about it. Helen phoned her the next day, and found it a great relief to talk to someone who knew what she'd been through.*

This example also illustrates a specific form of information: what somebody else did and felt in the same situation. In many crises this is helpful, reducing uncertainty and counteracting castastrophic thoughts.

The professional helper should always be on the look-out for opportunities to foster the individual's use of their social network. Indeed one can tackle this directly by helping the person map out their network, including weak bridging ties, and then discussing whose support can be enlisted for various kinds of help. The very act of listing all their potential supporters often reminds people of resources which, in the midst of the crisis, they had forgotten about.

In summary, skilled informative help is well-timed, if given when the person is receptive to new knowledge. It involves giving any information you have and, when you do not have it, acting as a link to sources of further information. Above all, it is about helping the person find out things for him- or herself as part of an active, problem-focused coping method.

COMPANIONSHIP

During and after crisis, we need people around us, not necessarily to give intense emotional support but just to engage with us in everyday social activities, sharing our ideas and memories, seeing things the same way as we do. This has the effect of re-establishing the social rules of the person's shattered world and provides validation to the self. It can also play a part in distraction, giving the person respite from intense negative feelings. This is one kind of help often available from the natural network. It can take the form of shared hobbies like jogging or music, but may just be spending time with someone, either quietly or in conversation. It is a different kind of help from intimacy or emotional support. Just as it is possible to have many casual friends and still feel lonely in the absence of an intimate tie, one can have a good intimate relationship and still need what friends and companions offer.

Whether this form of help is available in a crisis depends a great deal on the kind of social network that has been built up beforehand. Some people are very easy to get to know and are gregarious in their social world. Others have varying degrees of shyness, social anxiety, introversion and self-consciousness in relationships. Social anxiety tends to be combined with pessimism about the value of personal relationships and a lack of interest in other people's psychological problems. Socially anxious people can be so aware of their own feelings, and struggling so hard to think of what to say, that they fail to pay attention to the other person. They forget that the greatest social skill is to know how to listen. These social difficulties can inhibit the development of friendship, although some shared activities (for example, games like bridge and chess) place fewer demands on people to be socially competent since so much of the contact is rule-governed.

The amount of companionship available in crisis will therefore depend to quite a large extent on the personality of the individual and whether this has provided a network of friends. That said, people who report themselves as lonely do not necessarily have fewer friends than non-lonely people, but they do have different attitudes to these relationships.

PRACTICAL HELP

In the midst of crisis, practical help is needed and is often freely given. This can be straightforward and very tangible: cooking meals, doing washing, providing transport, looking after children, offering somewhere to stay, or lending money. Friends and family often provide an extraordinary level of practical help, to a degree which amazes the recipient and is deeply moving. We often say, in a crisis, 'Is there anything I can do?', and are delighted to find that there is, especially if the help needed is of this tangible, practical kind. In a way it is the easiest kind of help to give, because it does not require us to get too closely involved with the emotional pain: we can concentrate on the practical task and it gives us a role.

There are potentially two problems with practical help: first, when this is not what is really needed, but it is the only kind of help we know how to give; second, when we go on giving it past the point when the person should be doing things for him- or herself to regain a sense of independence and autonomy.

This is particularly the case with people who have suffered injury to body or brain resulting in a physical disability. In the later stage of this type of crisis, the individual will be struggling with the painful new reality that there are things he or she can no longer do and never will be able to. This requires learning to depend on others for some things. However, it equally requires learning to do as much as possible for oneself, and to re-establish self-respect and autonomy. In these stages of the crisis, helpers need to be able to give practical tasks back to the individual, even if it takes some patience and persistence to achieve this. Harm can be done by continuing to treat the disabled person as an ill person, an invalid.

PROFESSIONAL HELP – ENABLING OR DISABLING?

I have referred more than once to the ways in which professional helping differs from help given by friends and family. Many people safely negotiate their crises without ever seeing a professional, but it is in the nature of their work that professionals see many crisis sufferers. Seeing a small subgroup of those who are experiencing crisis and following them over a relatively brief time can lead us to generalise from this to crisis as a whole. I believe this has its dangers. Some professionals (the police, for example, or nurses and doctors in intensive care or burns units and casualty departments) tend to see people at their lowest ebb, when things are at their worst. Others (social workers and health visitors, for example) may see those who have the least effective coping strategies and have deficiencies in their natural support system. For all these reasons, we are apt to forget the positive side of the picture. Many people cope well with their crises, mobilise social support of varied kinds and learn a great deal from the experience. Our aim should be to promote this process in the people we are trying to help, and we should always remember that our help is only part of the picture. It is quite a skill to find an 'ecological niche' within the existing social networks from where we can influence people's coping methods and the way they mobilise other forms of help without disrupting or distorting natural helping processes.

What can go wrong? At worst, the professional can actually interfere with active coping and the use of natural systems of help.

▢ *A student in her early twenties was raped by a man who knew one of the friends with whom she shared a house. Although she had seen him a few times, on this occasion he turned up at the house when she was alone and forced himself on her. She was very frightened by his violence towards her and was in a state of shock and disbelief. Two days later she went to her doctor because she feared a pregnancy, but after explaining her experience she refused to undergo a vaginal examination, becoming very tearful and distressed. She did not want to go to the police, dreading a further degrading ordeal. The GP felt very sympathetic and wanted to help her. He asked her to come back to see him again the next day. During the next six weeks she saw him regularly, but during the talks she often fell silent whilst the doctor persisted with questions about the experience, her sexual history and later about her childhood. During this time she had stopped going to lectures, had withdrawn from the other people in the house, had told none of her friends – even her closest woman friend – about what had happened, and had not been in contact with the local rape-crisis centre.*

I have found that to be enabling rather than disabling requires us to relinquish the grandiose idea that 'Only I can help this person', or any variants on this. I need to accept with appropriate humility that I may not have much to offer, that I am not automatically the best person to help, and certainly that I am only part of a network of potential and actual helpers. I have to work from the assumption that the victim is an adult person, actively constructing his or her own reality, a person with the ability to learn from experience. This is different from seeing people as damaged objects that need repairing or as innocent victims of bad experiences or an oppressive social system.

There are paradoxes here. Humility about the limits of my impact does not preclude taking pride in my competence and developing my skills. Treating the person I am helping as an adult does not imply that I am blind to the needs and feelings of the child within them. Believing that people have the capacity to learn from experience should not stop me recognising when someone is clearly not doing so, but is repeating the same pattern over and over again. Ascribing active agency to someone does not mean that they have not been damaged or socially disadvantaged.

SELF-HELP GROUPS

Following a crisis, not all the help needed is necessarily available, either from the social network or from professional workers. Friends and family may fail to understand or may not have the knowledge needed. Professionals are in short supply, have limited time, and in any case can seem to inhabit a separate world. One way of providing emotional support, information, companionship and practical help is to form a new network where the members are not linked by ties of kinship or friendship (although friendships may flourish) but by the shared need for help with a particular problem. The enduring success of self-help groups has demonstrated the need for, and the value of, such networks. There are many such groups: for rape victims, bereaved people, parents with terminally ill children, HIV carriers and AIDS sufferers, victims of stroke or heart attack, and many more. A true *self*-help group is run by ordinary people for themselves. Sometimes a professional worker can have a valuable role as a back-up adviser or consultant. However, groups run by professionals to help crisis victims are not true self-help groups, although they sometimes become self-maintaining.

As well as providing many different types of help, these groups and networks empower people to take an active stance. They show what can be done by active problem-solving, and this can include fighting to change things.

BEING HELPED

So far I have concentrated on ways of helping someone suffering the effects of crisis, with the emphasis on what the helper can do. But helping is not a one-way process. In every helping action there must be two willing participants – the helper and the 'helpee', the recipient of help. Often, helping fails because the recipient does not want the help or is not able to use it. Some people are easy to help; they seem able to use what is offered. Others are difficult – nothing is quite right and the person trying to help them is left feeling very frustrated. Learning how to be helped is just as important as learning how to help. You can try Exercise 9, a quiz to tap attitudes to being helped, to see if you are an easy or a difficult person for others to help, then read why.

Being helped can be a humiliating experience. Some forms of help are more humiliating than others. These include help which is not freely given but which is in some way enforced, help which has to be asked for, help which has strings attached, help where there is no possibility of reciprocity, where the helper has a negative motive, and help which is greatly needed. These are kinds of help which would make most people feel uncomfortable. In contrast, spontaneously-offered help from someone who likes and respects you, whom you have helped in the past, who expects nothing in return, and where you could, if necessary, do without it, is much easier to accept graciously.

Unfortunately, it isn't as simple as this. Many kinds of help could give us negative messages about ourselves if we wanted to read them that way. Some people are more prone to humiliation than others. This is especially true when the crisis has produced a collapse of the usual sense of self. Sometimes, when fighting to preserve some image of the self as having power and control, accepting help can be too dangerous since it implies dependence and vulnerability. In this case a person will not seek help, and will reject it if it is offered. This can be their own coping strategy to defend themselves against the pain of humiliation, but it is a self-defeating one since it cuts off what humans in crisis need – human support.

Seeking help is only the beginning. Seeking the right help from the right people is very important. One of the blocks to being helped effectively is asking the wrong people for the wrong help. How can we judge this? Generally, it involves judging what it is reasonable to ask for, given the past history of your relationship, and which kind of help someone is realistically capable of giving.

There are two common difficulties here. First, there is the inappropriate request, such as asking someone to lend you a great deal of money during a first encounter or phoning one's ex-spouse, now remarried and living 50 miles away, at four o'clock in the morning wanting a shoulder to cry on. The second mistake is to ask for help from someone who does not have the capacity to give it, even if it is a reasonable

ATTITUDES TO BEING HELPED

EXERCISE 9

Do you agree or disagree with the following statements?

	Agree	Disagree
1. If you depend on other people for help they usually let you down.	☐	☐
2. When someone offers to help you, nine times out of ten they don't really mean it.	☐	☐
3. If people stood on their own feet more we'd all be better off.	☐	☐
4. I usually keep my troubles to myself, I don't like to worry my family about them.	☐	☐
5. When someone really loves you they know what you need without being told.	☐	☐
6. If you ask for help it can make people think less of you.	☐	☐
7. I like being the kind of person other people lean on.	☐	☐
8. I hate the thought of someone feeling sorry for me.	☐	☐
9. It's embarrassing to show someone else you need help.	☐	☐
10. I prefer to keep away from other people when I feel low.	☐	☐

How many times did you agree with these statements? More than three and you may be a difficult person to help!

request. A very common example of this is trying to get sensitive emotional support from someone who does not have the capacity to bear much emotion, is unskilled or uninterested in psychological matters, and is much better at practical or informative help. This latter error is doubly self-defeating, for one is not only refusing to consider alternative sources of emotional support but quite often rejecting the practical types of help that an emotionally insensitive person might be able and willing to give. Yet we often feel upset and disappointed because a particular person does not help in the way one feels he or she ought to.

Sometimes we fail to seek help because of a belief that the *only* kind of help which is of any value is quite spontaneous and unsolicited, and that asking for help is intrinsically humiliating. This attitude is guaranteed to fill us with bitterness and disappointment, since of course people are not mind-readers. In any case, this places the responsibility for helping entirely on the other person. Being helped is much easier if one is prepared to say what one needs.

If people refuse help because they fear humiliation, sometimes this refusal indicates an unwillingess to accept anything less than 'perfect' help. The ideal helper is highly empathic and always makes a perfect judgement about what is needed, then provides it. Right? Wrong! There is no such helper – this is a fantasy quite out of touch with what it means to be human. To be helped effectively, we have to know that other people will misjudge what we need, will let us down sometimes, will behave selfishly at times, will help us only in so far as it coincides with their own interests. We have to know this, tolerate it and accept it, because it does not mean that the help they *do* offer is not needed and not valuable.

One of the most difficult and painful things about being helped in a crisis is the feeling of shame at being in such a state and feeling unable to offer the helper anything in return. This feeling that the help is unbalanced can prevent someone accepting all they would like of what is offered. Quite correctly, we understand that helping and being helped constitute a social transaction and that there is a social norm of reciprocity about this exchange. There are several ways around this block to being helped. The first is to ask oneself this question: 'If our roles were reversed, would I do the same for this person?' Often the answer is 'Yes'. The second is to be aware that although this person is helping you, you may have helped others in the past or may be able to help them in the future in a similar non-reciprocal way. This can give a sense that there is an overall balance between what one takes and what one receives. Finally, we often forget that we always have access to one form of social 'payment' which is highly valued – gratitude.

Showing that one really appreciates what has been given is very important if you want to be the kind of person who is easy to help. Alas, the capacity to feel and show gratitude is diminished when there is a disturbance in the sense of self. Often we feel envy towards the person who is helping us – envy that they are not in this painful situation, that they have things we don't have. This feeling is not compatible with gratitude, since we secretly resent help from people we envy.

In short, we should value and use the help that people offer us. Sometimes people seek help but cannot use it. Sometimes they devalue the help that is available, or abuse their helpers by extorting more than they honestly feel able to give. This can seem puzzling until one remembers that the individual is behaving in this way because, from their point of view, it seems the best available option. The alternative, as they see it, may be worse. Many people believe that the alternative to perfect care is total abandonment. Some think that no help would be offered if they did not extort it. Others feel that the alternative to complete self-sufficiency is utter dependence. And so on. We probably all have some beliefs of this self-defeating nature, blocking us from receiving care. You may have found some of your own by doing the previous Exercise. The crisis reveals them, and provides both an opportunity and a motive to change them.

Chapter Six

Managing Stress

I have described the broad range of coping methods people use to work constructively with crisis, and ways they can be helped in this endeavour. In this chapter I am going to focus on specific techniques which have been developed to tackle stress directly. Crisis workers will benefit from being familiar with these, as they are all safe and quite simple but of well-established value. Before one can teach these methods to anyone else it is important to apply them to oneself. It is not only ironic if you are teaching stress management whilst being stressed yourself ('Do as I say, not as I do'); you will also be far less convincing or effective.

Stress is a normal part of everyday life and occurs whenever our bodies and minds are faced with demands which tax or exceed our capacity to respond. These demands can be physical (such as running uphill when not very fit) or mental (such as sitting an exam). All stress is actually both mental and physical, because the mind and the body are not separate but are two subsystems of one very complex whole. Stress originating in the mind, like an anxiety-provoking thought about a forthcoming exam, has bodily effects. (For full details of what everyday stress is and how to manage it, see another book in this series, *Managing Stress* by David Fontana.)

Crisis is very intense stress, so in addition to routine stress-management methods we need techniques to help with insomnia, nightmares and flashes of panic or despair. You also need to know when such problems have reached the point where it would be advisable to seek a specialist opinion. Some guidance about this is given at the end of the chapter.

TAKING CARE

People suffering severe stress need to give themselves all the care that they can. Unfortunately, they tend to do just the opposite. When in crisis we are prone to neglect the body's well-being as if it were just a machine which can be expected to go on working day after day, a mere vehicle for our preoccupied minds. The body in crisis is taking a lot of punishment, because it is constantly preparing to fight or to run away. As the system becomes flooded with stress hormones like adrenalin, the heart works faster, the muscles become fatigued, blood chemistry changes and toxins are not cleaned up as well as usual. Digestion is upset; and more often than not sleep, which is the usual time for the body to repair and restore itself, is badly disrupted too. Given all this, the body needs a helping hand during crisis. It certainly does not need any more trouble. Yet what do people characteristically do? Smoke more cigarettes and drink more alcohol and coffee, for a start. Usually we ask our bodies to deal with these poisonous substances because we find them pleasurable, and in crisis we use them in an attempt to regulate the distressing emotions. But there is no doubt that placing this extra burden on body chemistry under stress is adding to one's difficulties unnecessarily.

What can we do to help ourselves instead of making things harder? Bodily needs are basically simple – water, nutrients and oxygen. Most of us drink far less water than is good for us, and often we feed ourselves unwisely with too many fatty, salty and sugary low-fibre foods. Oxygen is in the air we breathe, but what kind of air is it and how do we breathe it? Is it stale, smoky air, full of exhaust fumes and other pollutants? Do we breathe deeply and easily, filling and emptying our lungs fully, or is it shallow breathing, using only the top third of our lungs?

Taking care of the body is not really difficult, but takes an effort at a time when one is utterly preoccupied with the painful crisis. It is worth reminding yourself, or the person with whom you are working, of some basics:

- Cut down on coffee, tea, beer, wine, spirits and smoking. If possible, cut them out altogether. Certainly don't consume any more than usual.

- Drink pure water – lots of it.

- Eat regular nutritious meals including fruit and vegetables.

- Get some form of regular exercise in fresh air.

THE ART OF RELAXATION

Crisis produces tension in the muscles. It is quite possible to be very tense indeed without realising it, and this causes many unpleasant problems: restlessness, tiredness, sleeplessness, headaches, back pain, lack of coordination. Together with the characteristic difficulties people have in concentrating following a crisis event, these contribute to the higher risk of having an accident at this time. Tackling muscle tension should always have a high priority.

Muscle tension can be reduced in many ways: for example, by exercising the muscles, being massaged, soaking in a warm bath. Swimming is excellent, as it combines exercise with the relaxing effects of water. In addition to these methods, learning to relax the muscles systematically is of great value. Some people think that relaxation just means sitting slumped in front of a television or putting one's feet up with a newspaper, but often the body is not relaxed at all during these activities. Nor is sleep necessarily relaxing. When under stress, it is possible for the muscles to remain tense, which leads to fitful, shallow sleep where one is tossing and turning all night. One can wake up feeling exhausted, with a clenched jaw or painful back and shoulders. Muscle relaxation is a learned skill, and like any skill it needs practice. When you start for the first time, it seems difficult; but, like riding a bicycle or learning to type, with practice it becomes automatic.

The relaxation exercise given here is based on the principle that you need to teach yourself the difference between a tense muscle and a relaxed one. In the first instance this means accentuating the tension in a particular muscle group, so that as you release it you can feel the sensation of relaxation. Deeper relaxation means letting that process continue. It is helpful to remember that one does not need to *do* anything to relax – one is simply *not* clenching the muscle. Since the clenching is unconscious and habitual, you need a conscious relearning process to stop doing it. To help you try the exercise, someone can read out the relaxation instructions in a calm and soothing voice. Equally effective is to record them on tape and play them back. (Just one word of warning: *never listen to a relaxation tape whilst driving a car.*) Try Exercise 10 – you'll feel good afterwards.

You will see that the relaxation exercise uses a mental cue, the word *relax*, which you say to yourself as you consciously unclench the muscles. It doesn't have to be this word – you can use any one you like. With repetition, this cue word becomes associated with the sensation of letting go of the tension. After a while the word alone will automatically produce the relaxation without any of the preliminaries. The mental

LEARNING TO RELAX

EXERCISE 10

▶ Settle back comfortably. Close your eyes and let yourself relax as much as you can. Listen to all the sounds you can hear and make a mental list of them. You'll be surprised how many different sounds there are. [*Pause*] Make sure your mental list is complete. Now, as you relax, clench your right fist. Just clench your fist tighter and tighter and notice the tension as you do it. Keep it clenched and feel the tension in your right fist and forearm . . . and now RELAX. Let the fingers of your right hand become loose and pay attention to the contrast in how it feels. Let yourself go, relax all over. Take a deep breath and let it out completely.

▶ Now repeat this with your left fist. Clench your left fist while the rest of your body stays relaxed; clench that fist tighter and tighter and study how tense and uncomfortable it feels . . . and now RELAX. Enjoy the feeling of the tension flowing away as you allow your hand and arm to relax. Your hand and arm are feeling heavier and more comfortable as the tension flows away. Continue to relax your whole body now. Take a deep breath and let it out completely. [*Pause*]

▶ Now clench both fists together and bend your elbows, making your biceps tense and tight as well . . . go on, clench your whole arms really tight, tighter and tighter, more and more tense . . . both fists tense, your forearms tense. Study the sensation . . . now, RELAX. Let your hands become loose and heavy, your arms heavy and relaxed. Feel the tension flow away and pay attention to how that feels. Continue to allow the relaxed heavy feeling to enter your body . . . more and more relaxed. Take a deep breath and let it out completely.

▶ Wrinkle up your forehead now; wrinkle it tighter . . . and now RELAX. Stop wrinkling your forehead, smooth it out. Picture your forehead and scalp becoming smoother and smoother as the relaxation continues. Next, frown . . . really frown, and crease your forehead and study the tense, tight sensation. . . . then RELAX. Let go of the tension, smooth out your forehead once more, feel it becoming more relaxed as the clenched tight feeling flows away and it is smoother and smoother. Now clench your jaws, bite your teeth together and put tension into your jaws and throat . . . now RELAX. Let your jaws become loose and relaxed, feel the tension flow away from your face; your forehead smooth, your scalp smooth and relaxed, your jaws relaxed and your throat unclenched, relaxed. Let the relaxation spread.

▶ Now pull in your stomach muscles, make them really tight and tense. That's it, make your abdomen hard and tight. Notice the tension . . . and RELAX. Let your tummy relax completely, allow the tension to flow out of your body and let the relaxation spread to your chest . . . shoulders . . . arms. Your whole body is now becoming more deeply relaxed as you let the tension go, allowing yourself to relax, to feel more deeply relaxed.

▶ Now flex your buttocks and thighs. Flex your thighs by pressing down on your heels as hard as you can. Feel the tight, hard, uncomfortable feeling in your thighs and buttocks. And now RELAX. Let the tension go. As you go on relaxing . . . notice the warm, heavy, comfortable feeling flowing into your body. Allow this relaxation to develop on its own. Just let yourself go and enjoy the difference between the tension and the relaxation.

▶ Breathing easily and naturally, let the unclenching continue, in your arms . . . shoulders . . . chest . . . stomach . . . thighs . . . calf muscles. Try and let go of all clenching anywhere in your body. Keep relaxing more and more deeply . . . more and more deeply, more deeply relaxed. Now you can become even more deeply relaxed. Just take a really deep breath . . . and let it out slowly . . . and RELAX. With your eyes closed, let all the muscles in your body become relaxed and heavy, heavy and relaxed. In a state of deep relaxation you feel unwilling to move a single muscle in your body. Think about the effort involved to raise your right arm. As you think about raising your arm, see if you notice any tension creeping into your shoulder and arm. Now you decide not to lift your arm but to continue relaxing. Feel the relief . . . the tension disappears . . . that's right . . . it's easy and comfortable to let yourself become deeply, completely, so deeply relaxed. Heavier and heavier . . . and more relaxed. As you lie there, breathing easily and naturally, you can enjoy the pleasant, warm, comfortable feeling flowing all over your body. Just carry on relaxing . . . [*Pause*]

When you want to get up, you can. Just count backwards from four to one. You should then feel fine and wide awake, calm and refreshed.

cue can be used in any situation where you find yourself clenching a muscle group. After practising the exercise regularly, you will be far more aware of which parts of your body are tensing up. To master the technique, most people need to practise it daily over a period of a fortnight.

INSOMNIA

Remember that some degree of insomnia is perfectly normal after a severe stress event. The mind/body system is alert; nervous energy is aroused; and a great deal of information processing is going on. This makes sleep less likely; and if one does sleep, one is more likely to be aware of dreams, some of which will be frightening. These are normal processes. It is important not to think of insomnia during a crisis as an illness or disorder to be treated immediately with sleeping pills. The problem with these drugs is that they do not help the body re-establish its own rhythm of natural sleep. If taken regularly and over a long period, sleeping pills can actively prevent this happening, past the point where the crisis stress itself has begun to recede and sleep would normally be re-established. It is even possible that such drugs inhibit the information-processing function of dreaming, so working against constructive crisis resolution. Having said this, people have found that the *short-term* use of sleeping pills can prevent total exhaustion and break a vicious circle: sleeplessness leading to worry about not sleeping, which in turn prevents sleep. One must weigh up the costs and benefits, but in any case there is nothing to be lost by trying natural methods first. For many people psychological techniques, such as deep muscle relaxation and control of worry, prevent exhaustion and make drugs unnecessary.

The most important thing with insomnia in crisis is not to worry about it. Sleep is one of the bodily functions which we cannot consciously will – in fact, the more you try to force yourself to go to sleep, the less able you will be to do it. It is a matter of acceptance, since sleep can happen only when one lets go of conscious striving. Sleep involves relinquishing the wakeful mind, not using it to try to sleep. If one is taking care of the body with the methods discussed so far, one can manage with very little sleep, much less than you might expect. Furthermore, even if you feel you haven't slept a wink all night, the chances are that you have in fact been asleep during some intervals. This difference between subjective and objective sleep has been well established in the sleep laboratory. Although it is annoying to think that you might be asleep whilst believing you are awake, it does mean that your body is geting some sleep and can continue to function.

The biggest problem with insomnia is that we work ourselves up into a state about it. Perhaps you have had the experience of lying awake, looking at the clock every hour or so, thinking 'This is terrible. I must go to sleep. If I don't, how am I going to manage tomorrow?' Every so often you might enter a twilight half-sleep, but with the same kinds of worries and thoughts still going round and round. If this continues for several nights, it starts to establish a habit and you need to retrain your sleep pattern.

There are two kinds of sleep disturbance. In the first, described above, it is impossible to get to sleep in the first place. Silly or worrying thoughts go round and round; in fact one's mind can be racing like an engine out of gear. In the second kind of insomnia, one can fall asleep all right but then wake up two or three hours later and find it hard to drop off again.

There are some very simple rules for handling insomnia of both kinds. First of all, it is very important to establish that going to bed means going to sleep. A strong habitual association between the two makes sleep more automatic. Most people with a sleep problem have reversed this, so that bed is associated with restlessness. How do you retrain yourself? Go to bed when you feel sleepy, not until, and lie quietly. *Do not try to go to sleep.* Paradoxically, it is sometimes better to say to yourself 'Whatever happens, don't go to sleep just yet.' Just do the relaxation exercise described in the previous section feeling that warm, heavy, comfortable sensation flowing from your feet, through your legs, over your tummy, into your shoulders and arms and finally your neck, scalp, face and jaw. Keep clearing the fretful thoughts from your mind (more on this later). If after an hour you are still not asleep, *get up.* Do not lie there awake for hours on end. Go downstairs or into another room and read a book, stroke the cat, listen to music, do the washing-up, do anything. When you actually feel sleepy – and do not force yourself – go back to bed and repeat the relaxation procedure.

The same principle applies to waking up in the night. The first thing is to make sure that the muscles are relaxed *before* going to sleep. Then, if you wake up, lie quietly, relaxing the muscles and clearing worries from your mind. If after an hour you are still awake, get up.

I have mentioned the importance of clearing the mind of worries and fretful thoughts. These thoughts are a major reason for insomnia. Often something that would not worry you in the clear light of day can, during that twilight half-sleep, loom up out of all proportion as a dreadful problem. It is possible to learn to control these worries. First you must accept that you can have some choice over whether or not your mind fills up with this kind of thought. It is not a question of fighting the thoughts but gently, persistently, putting them aside, removing your attention from them. Of course, they will come crowding back; but as often as they do, you clear them away again. Most people find emptying the mind completely a very difficult thing. It is easier to focus attention on something positive. Here there is a wide choice of options. Counting sheep is the traditional one! Possibly better is a visual image of a cloudless horizon, perhaps over the sea. As each worrying thought comes up, think of it as a cloud on the horizon and gently push it away until the sky is clear again. There are many other visual images to choose from, according to your own preference. These might include: lying on a sandy beach hearing the waves gently and rhythmically breaking on the shore; watching the rain steadily and gently falling on to a lake; flying low and silently over hills, forests and dales; sitting by a river watching it flow; walking through a beautiful garden full of delightful things (although keen gardeners should beware of starting to worry about the best placing of the plants or what to do about the ground elder). All these images give a restful and wholesome focus for the mind, as an alternative to the internal chatter of anxiety, the junk mail of the mind. Another useful method is to focus one's attention of a particular place in the body – for example, feeling the breath entering and leaving your body through the nostrils. Each time a worry pops up, gently remove your attention from it and back to the breath entering and leaving, entering and leaving. Do not get annoyed if you have to do this repeatedly; as often as you need to, you can clear aside the worry and refocus your attention.

The next part of tackling insomnia is a very difficult one for many people, although it is quite simple: *get up at the same time each morning*, even if you have fallen asleep only an hour before. This seems very cruel when you have finally dropped off, but it is essential in establishing a sleep rhythm. It even applies at weekends, at least until your insomnia is a thing of the past. The same principle applies to the next rule: *do not take catnaps during the day.* Many people who cannot sleep during the night take an afternoon nap. This fuels the problem by disrupting the night-time sleep rhythm further. Daytime naps, whilst pleasurable, are a luxury for those who can sleep at night or a necessity for those who have other reasons for not sleeping – elderly people or those nursing young babies. They are not a good idea for insomniacs.

Anyone with a sleep problem should cut out caffeine, since this is a stimulant and works against sleeping properly. This is a simple step, but you might be surprised at the difference it makes. Similarly, alcohol, although it can help you fall asleep, is likely to cause you to wake up shortly afterwards. If you do drink some alcohol in the evening, drink plenty of pure water before going to bed.

NIGHTMARES

Nightmares are a common form of sleep disturbance after a severe stress event. If the individual has been exposed to trauma, as in a car accident or major disaster, dreaming about it is part of the normal reprocessing that the mind uses to make sense of what has happened. These are not strictly nightmares but a sleeping form of flashback experience. Nightmares have an element of horror which is beyond reality.

❏ *A young man's father died of cancer. They had always been very close, and he felt shocked and numb. Without discussing it, his father had asked to be cremated after death. This came as a surprise to him, and afterwards he felt that his father had disappeared completely. One night he dreamt that he looked out of the window and saw his youngest child in the garden. She was striking matches and watching them burn. He called to her to take care and started banging in the window but could not prevent his little girl catching fire. She was running round the garden with her clothes alight and her father couldn't help her. He could see her face contorted with pain and woke up yelling out in horror.*

This kind of nightmare can be seen as part of the mind's effort to process the full emotional implications of the bereavement. In the dream are elements of fire, death, fear, helplessness, a child in danger, a father's inability to protect or save, being cut off from someone loved, and so on. Because these preoccupations arouse so much anxiety, the dream is not only remembered (whereas normally most dreams are forgotten) but indeed wakes up the dreamer. Nightmares can become a problem when they are recurrent and thus produce a phobic response. This adds to daytime anxiety, and at night the anticipatory anxiety can make one dread going to sleep.

If a particular nightmare is having this effect, the way forward is not to try and forget it but to find a good listener and tell him or her the whole dream in as much detail as possible, more than once. If you are helping a nightmare sufferer, encourage the person to relate the dream to you *several times*. This will arouse a good deal of anxiety; but persevere, since it is exposure to this anxiety which will reduce it. With each rehearsal of the horrifying scene, its power to create fear diminishes as it becomes clearly 'only a dream' and not a dangerous, harmful thing.

CONTROLLING PANIC

Moments of intense anxiety which may amount to panic are often experienced during or following crisis. The first thing to understand about anxiety and panic is that they are not in themselves harmful or dangerous. Healthy people do not die of panic attacks. The sensations of hot dizziness and a thumping heart are very unpleasant indeed, but not in themselves cause for alarm. It is even true to say that most of us lead very sedentary lives in which we would be healthier if we took exercise to make our hearts beat fast for two or three minutes each day. The heart can pound with no ill effects at all.

As explained in Chapter 2, panic is a vicious circle of anxiety about anxiety which results in hyperventilation and over-arousal of the sympathetic nervous system. In order to control panic, it is necessary to equip oneself with three skills – relaxation (already described), a slow-breathing technique, and a method for controlling anxious thoughts.

Over-breathing is a fast, shallow breathing which uses only the top part of the lungs (breathing from the chest) rather than the diaphragm, the large muscle at the bottom of the chest cavity, which inflates the whole lung (breathing from the abdomen). This form of shallow breathing, like muscle tension, can become habitual and unconscious. To be well prepared for panic, it is good to recognise this type of breathing and to substitute a slow form. Try an exercise:

▶ *Put one hand on your diaphragm (on the midriff under the ribs) and the other on the top of your chest. Take a deep, slow breath in to the count of five, and then let it all out equally slowly to the count of five. Breathe so that you can feel your higher hand stay still whilst your lower hand moves. Try it. IN – one – two – three – four – five – hold – OUT – one – two – three – four – five. Repeat twice more, then breathe normally.*

Practising this exercise daily when you are not in a panic will help you to recall the correct kind of breathing when you need it.

Controlling anxious thoughts is very worthwhile. People tend to believe that they are powerless in the face of these thoughts, as if they had no choice over what to think. This part of panic control involves rejecting this point of view and deciding that you are going to think what *you* want to think, not have the anxiety push frightening thoughts into your mind. Even if such thoughts arrive in your mind, you have a choice whether or not to believe them. Agreed, the thought 'I'm having a heart attack' can be pretty convincing when you feel hot, dizzy and sick, and your heart seems to be bursting out of your chest and missing beats into the bargain. This is why one has to prepare more helpful alternative thoughts in advance, and have them ready. If necessary, the panic sufferer can write these alternative thoughts on to cards and carry them around. When the panic feeling comes on, he or she should take them out and read them whilst practising slow breathing. Here are some suggestions for benign alternatives to the panicky thoughts:

▶ *This is an attack of anxiety. It will wash over me, reach a peak, and then go away again. It will not harm me. If I sit quietly and breathe slowly I will feel better soon. It's like a wave of unpleasant feelings but I will come through it all right. I am doing very well, just letting it happen. Breathe slowly and let all the air out before taking another breath. Relax the muscles and just let it happen. Just stay with it. I can cope with this. Nothing terrible is going to happen to me.*

This train of thought will allow the panic attack to fade away quite quickly, because it does not keep fanning the flames of fear. What is equally important, it gives the individual the experience of successfully coping with the panic without fleeing from the situation. This reduces future anxiety levels in the same situation. It takes some practice to be able to keep these benign thoughts in one's mind during the panic itself. That is why it is important to do some practising before the attack happens. Then it is much easier, because you know what to expect and have the antidote ready. These techniques *work* if applied conscientiously. No one can make panic enjoyable or remove it by magic. These methods simply make it bearable, and eventually the frequency and intensity of the attacks will reduce.

TACKLING DEPRESSION

The crisis may have brought loss of one kind or another, of which the natural consequence is a lowered mood state. Frightening experiences can also produce depressed mood as a secondary effect of the anxiety. Much loss or injury has a normal phase of depression as part of the work of grieving discussed in Chapter 2. Is there anything people can do to help themselves during this time?

The first thing is not to expect too much of oneself. 'Normal' depression following a life-transforming event is a state of lowered activity which has the function of protecting the self from further injury, conserving resources and allowing recovery to take place. Crying is a natural part of it, so don't be ashamed about having a good cry. Sometimes, weeping or sobbing can be a great relief, for after the pain of loss is experienced fully there is often a natural numbness or lifting of mood when the other side of the picture is restored.

Other aspects of depression include feeling tired, slowed down in one's thoughts and actions, and not being able to concentrate very well. These symptoms are to be expected during a depressed phase, and it is very important to recognise them as part of the depression rather than blaming oneself. For example, a depressed person will not be able to do all the things he or she normally does at work with the same degree of competence. One has to allow oneself longer to get things done and expect to do fewer things. This does not mean one is going to be in this state for ever. As the depression lifts, a more usual level of ability will return. Until then it is pointless berating oneself or making oneself feel bad about it. The depressed person should do everything possible to reduce the level of demand to a point at which they can manage successfully. Most jobs have some leeway for 'freewheeling' for a while.

The next thing you can help someone to do is to note fluctuations in mood state. The person can keep a note of any times the depression is worse than others. It may have a regular daily rhythm, but quite often the individual will notice that certain events can trigger off an episode of depressed feeling. It is worth keeping track of what these are. For example:

A university teacher decided to retire in her early fifties to set up her own business, despite her husband's misgivings. The first year was quite hard, but she felt optimistic and was enjoying her work. Suddenly her mother, who was a widow in her eighties, died of a stroke. She found herself very low indeed after the death. Once, she tried to talk to her husband about how she was feeling but he seemed quite unsympathetic, perhaps because he had never liked her mother. He seemed to imply that she was making too much of it; he had lost his own mother years before, and had not made such a fuss over it. During the next few weeks she found it harder and harder to keep things going in the business. She realised that her depressed feelings were strongest whenever she had gone to see a new client to sell her services. Each time, the next day she felt very sluggish and down, hardly wanting to get out of bed. Thinking about this, she wrote down all the thoughts that were in her mind just as they occurred to her. She realised that she felt like a fraud, an impostor. The thoughts in the back of her mind which preceded the depression were variations on the theme 'You've got nothing to offer, and it's only a matter of time before they find out'.

Why is this kind of discovery useful? It shows us that the depression is not arbitrary, just arriving like bad weather to be tolerated and endured. Depression is often a result of things we tell ourselves. This particular woman was quite surprised to find she was undermining herself in this way, because when she thought about it rationally she knew she did have a lot to offer and was not defrauding anyone. Her mother's death and the feeling of being let down by her husband have combined to produce a crisis of self-confidence. The depression of grief is, perfectly normally, reducing her capacity to work efficiently. She has then gone on to interpret this as evidence that she is an impostor.

Many mood fluctuations are caused by a hidden thought of this kind. Often, by keeping a diary of mood changes, it is possible to discover the depressing or upsetting thought which is nagging away. Then you have the possibility of choice. You are not forced to believe this thought if there are more objective alternative ones which will lead to other ways of feeling.

Keeping a mood diary also reminds you of good days, times when some things go well and there are pleasures and satisfactions. Setting out to do something each day which gives satisfaction of this kind is well worthwhile. As well as the trap of depressed thinking leading to more depression, the lack of motivation to get out and do anything can reduce the potential for pleasures and rewards which might offset the depressed mood. This is why many people are helped through their depression by having a routine which they are obliged to maintain even if they do not particularly feel like it. This is why, so long as workload demands can be reduced to a realistic level, it is often very valuable to continue in one's job through a depression rather than take extended leave. Animals can also provide routine. Many people find that their cat, dog, or even the budgie provides comfort and companionship and a requirement to continue to care for them.

Imagery can help in depressed episodes. The visual metaphor has a power to reach the unconscious part of the mind. After completion of the relaxation procedure described in Exercise 10, a further script can be added to the tape which helps to focus quite deep-level thoughts on the possibility of a future. You will probably be able to think of your own images, but here is one possibility which has been found helpful:

▶ *Imagine you are walking deep into a forest in winter. It is very cold and bleak. The trees are all bare, wet and black. The sky is dark-grey, heavy with unfallen snow, and there is a cold wind. The ground underneath your feet is sodden with dead leaves. As you walk deeper into the forest, it seems to get colder and colder. You walk into a clearing and sit on the trunk of a fallen tree. It is very quiet. Looking down at your feet, you notice a layer of bracken. Reaching down and moving it aside, you see three small green shoots just beginning to push themselves up. Then you can imagine what it is like to be a bulb lying under the cold, wet soil in the winter. The bulb lies there, dormant, not using up any energy and at this time seeming utterly lifeless. But the potential for growth and life is deep inside it, waiting for the sunshine and warmth to return. Safe under the earth, not impatient, just waiting. The whole forest, so bleak and lifeless, knows that spring will return, although those long dark days seem as if they will go on for ever and that it will never come. But it will come.*

WHEN IS SPECIALIST HELP NEEDED?

These ways of helping someone cope with crisis stress are not particularly complicated but are based on sound psychological principles. Crisis can lead to the point where stress triggers a more severe and intractable problem than you can cope with yourself. There are no rigid rules for when to seek a specialist opinion, since a great deal depends on the level of social support available and the capacity of the individual to tolerate a particular level of distress. Here are some guidelines, though, about how to recognise when someone needs the help of a mental health specialist. (The general practitioner can then make a referral to a psychiatrist or chartered clinical psychologist.)

- Depressed mood has been intense and unfluctuating for more than two weeks, so that the individual has been unable to enjoy anything.

- There are recurrent thoughts of suicide or there have been plans made to carry this out.

- Depressed mood is accompanied by all of the following: loss of interest in previously enjoyed activities, social withdrawal, hopelessness about the future, concentration difficulties, and exhaustion.

- Depressed mood is accompanied by appetite loss, guilt, being very slowed down, and waking early in the morning.

- There have been four or more panic attacks within a month.

- Routine activities like shopping, going to work, or travelling on public transport are being avoided due to anxiety.

— RESPONDING TO A — COMPLEX CRISIS

EXERCISE 11

At this stage it is worth returning to Exercise 4 – the chemist who was a compulsive gambler.

After reading Chapter 3 you were in a position to unravel the strands of his complex crisis in order to draw yourself a mental map of what was happening. Now you should be able to go further and think of a range of coping strategies, forms of help and stress-management skills which would be likely to foster a resolution of the crisis.

Go back now to page 42 and read the vignette again, then reread your own notes on the crisis. Now make two lists.

▶ First, using the information in Chapters 4–6, write down all the things you think he could do to cope constructively with the crisis.

▶ Next, write down what you think his manager could do to help him achieve a constructive response.

After you have done this, you may be interested to compare your notes with mine on p.115; but, as before, this is for interest and guidance only – these are not the only or necessarily the right answers.

Chapter Seven

Life After Crisis

We can now see that a crisis is not a single event. The word stands for a series of processes over time, and a crisis has a beginning, a middle and an end, with different issues at each stage. The event triggering the crisis first leads to shock and numbness, then an emotional realisation of what has happened. This leads to feelings of anxiety, angry protest and sometimes, later, depression. The individual makes efforts to cope with both the crisis situation and the crisis emotions. Sometimes this coping is successful; but if it fails, there is increased distress and a mobilisation of more social or internal resources. Often this contains and resolves the crisis; but if this second line of action fails, a third threshold of distress is reached, when professional help is sought. At some stage there is a resolution and a process of rebuilding. You may be involved with someone's crisis at any point in this process. Mental health professionals tend to be formally involved later rather than sooner in many crises. However, many other professional workers, in the nature of their jobs, will find themselves involved at the earlier stages.

Seeing someone during crisis is like glimpsing one snapshot from a photograph album of a whole life. Because different professional workers encounter an individual for short periods throughout the crisis and its aftermath, it is difficult to form a picture of its place in the person's whole life. Understanding the current picture in terms of the person's biography is very illuminating. This chapter will try to provide this picture by demonstrating how a crisis is woven into the fabric of a person's life and will continue to have effects – for good or ill – years later. It will also describe the role played by professional workers in helping people at various stages of the crisis. In this sense, although there are many similarities between situations and one can work from basic principles, every crisis is unique because every person is unique. Although it is possible to list the major life crises (loss of a spouse, other bereavement, serious illness or injury to self or loved one, and so on), each time a crisis happens it happens anew.

THE NEGATIVE RESOLUTION

Crises will resolve for better or worse. The crisis may be over, but the individual can be left unwell or unable to deal with future life demands. The effects of a crisis which has been poorly resolved can be very far reaching. Many of the people seeing doctors, psychologists, counsellors and psychotherapists because of mental health problems can trace their difficulty to a much earlier crisis which has not been worked through properly.

☐ *Ann and Robert were eagerly awaiting the birth of their first child. Everything had been prepared; the baby's room was ready, and they had taken great pleasure in choosing clothes and toys. The birth was long and difficult. After a night and a day of contractions, Ann was very tired, and the midwife acted swiftly when the baby's heartbeat slowed down and the head stopped making progress. A doctor arrived and Robert was asked to leave as they prepared for a forceps delivery. Suddenly the room seemed to fill with strange people. Ann was very disorientated and confused, both from the pain and the medication. It seemed an eternity before the baby was delivered; then the room emptied and only one student midwife was left with her, who said they were looking after the baby and someone would come to stitch her up soon. Her husband didn't reappear until one hour later. They couldn't find out what was happening. Although people were kind and efficient in helping her get clean and return to the ward, no one would say very much.*

Much later, after Robert had gone home to get some sleep, an unfamiliar doctor came on to the post-delivery ward and sat on Ann's bed. She said that there had been some complications; baby had had a difficult time and needed to rest. He was being cared for in the special-care baby unit, and she could see him the next day.

It was almost a week before the couple were told that their baby had suffered brain damage during birth and that he would not grow up normally. No one seemed willing to say just what the extent of the damage was, why it had happened, or to commit themselves on exactly the extent of the problems he was likely to have. One doctor called Robert into the corridor and said in a low voice, 'He many never be able to walk or talk, but I might be wrong. We just have to wait and see.'

In the following weeks, the couple found it very difficult to talk to each other about what had happened. Ann couldn't understand why Robert had abandoned her during labour and had not returned for so long. He couldn't explain his own ordeal of pacing the corridor, seeing the team rush off with the baby, not knowing what was happening. He had desperately wanted to go back into the delivery room but was frightened. He didn't feel assertive enough just to walk in without permission. He was now ashamed of this and couldn't handle Ann's angry criticism. Nor could they speak about their disappointment and grief at not having the normal baby they had been expecting. Robert didn't want anything to do with the baby, and wanted Ann to agree that he should be looked after in hospital, but she insisted on bringing him home as soon as she could.

Less than a year later, after many bitter arguments and recriminations, their marriage broke up. Ann and the baby went to live at her parents' home. Robert lived alone in the house for a while. He saw his old friends quite a lot, going with them to pubs and motor-bike rallies. He had some one-night stands and started to drink very heavily. A year later he lost his job, and shortly afterwards was referred to the local alcohol unit.

Ann and Robert were unlucky. First, their normal baby was damaged by an unpredicted set of birth complications. Second, none of the midwives or doctors involved gave immediate crisis support. The professional workers did not 'stay with' Ann and Robert emotionally, partly because they were busy with the urgent technical details of saving the baby's life but also because they themselves felt very anxious. Later on, bad news was broken to one partner rather than both; the information given was incomplete; and there was no follow-up to discuss things properly at a time when they could have understood it. No one in their social network recognised that a grieving process was involved, that the couple needed to mourn the loss of the normal child they had wanted. None of the many professionals with whom the couple came into contact in the following weeks provided an opportunity for them to talk to each other openly.

The crisis has revealed a vulnerability in their relationship which has its roots in the past. As a result of childhood experiences, Ann has always been very sensitive to the feeling of being let down, reacting angrily and intolerantly to anyone not meeting her needs or living up to her expectations. Robert's difficulty is that he finds it hard to deal with criticism. His automatic reaction when criticised is to flare up and reject the other person completely, as a way of protecting himself from the pain of rejection. In routine, non-stressful circumstances this did not cause them many problems, just a few arguments which they managed to patch up. What happened at the hospital though, in the context of their crisis responses (problems with thinking clearly, anxiety, and negative thoughts), has challenged the ability of their relationship to contain negative feelings. The crisis has aroused childlike anxieties. Ann reacts with hurt and anger to Robert, as if he is an abandoning, neglectful parent; Robert sees

Ann as a critical, unfairly-judging parent and moves into rebellion. They begin to see each other as enemies. They are not able to mobilise the resources within themselves or their network to tackle this problem.

As well as this, information on which to base decisions about caring for their baby was not easily available. The hospital staff did not offer them an appointment to explore the full implications of bringing up a child with severe learning difficulties and physical disabilities. They were not enabled to make a positive decision together based on a reasoned appraisal of the full range of possibilities.

From this one crisis, badly handled, a number of other problems developed. The specific crisis of the baby's birth was resolved by Ann and Robert's avoidance of the issues it raised within their relationship: the nature of their marital commitment in the face of mutual disappointment, anger and a sense of grievance. The resolution enabled Ann to transfer her commitment to her baby, whom she loved and was determined to care for whatever happened. The baby will always need her and she will never be an abandoning parent. Robert was left, in this instance, without a parental role or a marriage. He returned to the pursuits of his adolescence, and, due to further avoidance through alcohol abuse, was also left without a job.

THE POSITIVE RESOLUTION

This illustration shows why helping people work through crisis to a deeper, more lasting resolution is uniquely valuable: not only does it prevent the development of further problems, but the experience provides the individuals concerned with the knowledge that they are capable of facing painful adversity and finding a way through it. This enhances their self-esteem and makes future crisis more manageable. Is it possible for professional workers to respond more helpfully?

❑ *The sister on the burns unit was an experienced specialist nurse, but even so she felt herself tense up inside when she saw the small child's injuries. There were severe burns to her face, neck and chest after the toddler had pulled a pan of boiling oil over herself. The sister knew she would be ill for a long time, with the regular torture of dressings being changed, and later a number of operations to graft skin on to her face. When the immediate medical and nursing procedures were complete, she went outside and found the child's mother, who was sitting in the corridor, staring into space. She went up to the woman and sat next to her for a moment before saying quietly, 'Mrs Jones, I'm Jan Smith. We're looking after Amy now. Let's go somewhere we can talk.' Beth Jones looked up at her as if she had not heard her and said, 'It's incredible. I was only out of the kitchen for a second. I didn't think she could reach up that far. I just can't believe it.' She covered her face with her hands and started to tremble. 'Oh my God, it's terrible! How can I tell Frank?' Sister Smith laid a hand on Mrs Jones's arm: 'You've had a very bad shock, Mrs Jones. Amy has had an accident and I'm here to help you. We can phone your husband from my office. Will you come with me?'*

Jan arranged for a cup of tea with sugar to be brought for Mrs Jones and made sure they would not be interrupted. She spent half an hour listening to what had happened, letting her talk and cry freely. After a while Beth asked if she could phone her husband, and Jan left her alone to do this, returning to find her calmer and ready to give her the basic information she needed. 'When Frank arrives I'll leave you alone together for a while. Then I've arranged for the doctor to come and speak to you both together. You can ask him any questions you like. Don't worry if you can't remember everything you wanted to ask, you'll have another talk with the doctor the day after tomorrow. The main thing to remember is that Amy's in the best possible place to be cared for. She will come through this.' 'Can I see her just for a minute before Frank gets here?' Jan could read fear as well as longing in the mother's eyes. 'Yes, of course. I'll come with you. You'll find she won't wake up because she's had something to make her sleep. She has bandages on her face and there is a drip in her arm.'

This illustrates some helpful ways of dealing with the immediate crisis. The sister knows that the mother needs to talk about what happened and her feelings, but she also knows that the corridor is not the right place to do this. She speaks quietly and is patient, repeating herself if necessary and not expecting the mother to take in what she says all at once. She recognises the initial stage of crisis – shock. She makes it easy for Beth to phone her husband but she does not rush to do it, giving an opportunity first for her to confide if there is any reason why this is especially difficult (for example, the husband may not be the child's own father or there may be a marital estrangement). She allows free expression of the feelings without getting upset herself. Above all, she adjusts her pace and responses to the needs of the person in crisis. She arranges for a doctor to speak to them both, but only after they have had some privacy together. She anticipates that at this stage they will be too numb to take in what has happened, or its implications. Therefore she does not try to give much information, except that which is absolutely central (that Amy is receiving the best care and that she will survive). For the same reason, she makes sure that the couple have another chance to talk to a doctor two days later. By this time they will be much more able to take in information and will have questions of their own. Finally, she responds positively to the request to see the child, but accompanies her and tells her what to expect. Preparing the mother in this way lessens the shock of seeing the little girl enclosed in dressings, unconscious, with tubes attached to her.

This kind of crisis response is very facilitating. Months later, when the couple have mobilised many of the resources of their social network and are coping with the medium-term crisis effects, Beth often remembers with gratitude the gentle voice and the hand on her arm. She remembers vividly Jan's words: 'Amy has had an *accident* and I'm here to help you.' This meant a great deal to her later: from the tone of voice as well as the words themselves, she could tell that the sister was not blaming her. Through the difficult days that followed, Beth found that Jan could always be relied on to be calm and to find some time to listen. For example, she helped Beth to talk about how she could hardly bear to see Amy after the burns-dressing procedure, when the little girl was so very distressed and sometimes would turn away from her mother. Beth talked about how rejected and guilty she felt at these moments. This helped her a great deal in staying with Amy, in accepting the reality of her pain without withdrawing from her emotionally.

The other person who helped Beth and Frank was the health visitor. She visited them at home and gave them helpful background information about the frequency of accidents in the home, which made them realise how common they were. She also explained in more detail the things that the doctors had told them at the hospital. Finally, she helped them to talk to each other about what had happened.

❏ *From the beginning, Frank had not wanted to know the full details of what had happened. He would not talk about it, saying only that it was over and done with and that they had to face the future, not go over the past. One evening they had an argument about something else when they were both pretty angry. In the midst of this, Frank said, 'Amy wouldn't be where she is now if you'd been doing your job properly'. Although he apologised later and said he didn't mean it, Beth was very hurt and withdrew from him. She told the health visitor why they were not speaking to each other. The health visitor arranged to see the two of them together the following evening, and with her help they were able to express their feelings to each other: first, mutual anger, then Beth spoke of her remorse and guilt. For the first time she told Frank exactly what had happened, and how she had been haunted by nightmares and flashbacks which she had not been able to tell him about. Frank was able to speak about his own distress and his fears for the future.*

This health visitor has enabled the couple to get beneath the surface of their angry feelings and explore some of the hurt and fear underneath. This discussion helps them to start to confide in each other. In the past, even before the crisis, each partner had tended to respond to stress by withdrawing into his or her own feelings. For the first time, as a result of these events, the young couple began to learn how to listen to each other. It was by no means a straightforward or rapid process, but years afterwards they were able to see that their relationship 'grew up' significantly at this point.

TAKING THE LONG-TERM VIEW

These examples demonstrate practically what was discussed more theoretically in Chapter 3: that many crises will activate significant long-term issues for individuals and their relationships, and the way these issues are handled can be crucial for their future well-being. It is very tempting, when working with someone in crisis, to deal with the immediate problems without thinking too much of the long term. After all, there is plenty happening to engage one's attention. Effective crisis work does address short-term problems, but always keeps in sight the life span issues to which they relate. It is only later that the full significance of the crisis will become apparent to the people caught up in it. At the time, it is very difficult to judge whether a particular event or difficulty will turn out later to have been a valuable experience. The crisis worker should not judge this in advance but should keep an open mind about it. This does not mean making trite comments such as 'You may find later this is a blessing in disguise'. These remarks are completely unhelpful to someone in the throes of crisis. What matters is the crisis worker's *own understanding* of the ways in which a crisis can act as a force for development, leading to greater personal fulfilment in the long run. It is the worker's own internal map of crisis in its long-term effects which enables him or her to open up to whatever the person is experiencing without feeling hopeless, frightened or overwhelmed.

Do you think your own internal map of crisis has been developed by reading this book? One way to check this, out of interest, is to do Exercise 12, which is a repeat of the 'Attitudes to Crisis Quiz' (Exercise 1). You might find you have changed some of your ideas. It is worth thinking through in what ways you do see things differently. If you have not changed your attitudes, again it is worth thinking why not. Is it that you were already well informed about crisis before you started? Remember that you can try the quiz again in the future, perhaps after some practical work with someone in crisis – yourself, a friend, a colleague or a client.

IN CONCLUSION

At the beginning I said that this would not be a book of rules or guidelines for what to do and what not to do in working with crisis, but rather an exploration of the psychology of crisis to help the reader deepen and broaden their understanding of these human processes. This is because I believe we work better, more sensitively and more

ATTITUDES TO CRISIS QUIZ REASSESSED

EXERCISE 12

Do not look at your previous answers. As before, give each item a score from 1 to 5 on the following scale:

1 = Definitely no, I disagree strongly.
2 = No, I disagree.
3 = I don't feel strongly one way or the other.
4 = Yes, I agree.
5 = Yes, definitely. I agree strongly.

1. It is always better to avoid a crisis if you can. ☐
2. People usually make their own crises. ☐
3. Crises just happen, often there is nothing you can do to prevent them. ☐
4. It takes about three months to recover from a bereavement. ☐
5. It is best to try and take your mind off things if you are feeling very upset. ☐
6. There is always something to be learned from a crisis. ☐
7. Once a person is very anxious or depressed, there is not much they can do about it themselves. ☐
8. If someone is experiencing horrifying 'flashbacks' to a crisis event it means they are suffering from a post traumatic stress disorder. ☐
9. Professional health workers generally know how to handle a crisis. ☐
10. You are more likely to have an accident following a stressful event. ☐
11. Professional help is usually needed if someone has had a severely stressful event. ☐
12. After most crises it is best to get things back to normal as quickly as possible. ☐
13. It's just a matter of luck if you get the right kind of help during a crisis. ☐
14. Crisis is what happens when your emotions get out of control. ☐

When you have completed the quiz, for each item separately subtract this score from the previous one. Ignore the minus signs and add up the differences. The total is a measure of how much you have changed your views. On this type of quiz, a total difference score of 10 is a considerable change, less than 3 is very little change. You might be interested to see my answers to the questions on page 112.

flexibly, from an internal map of the subject rather than following a set of rules, like a recipe. Although I have kept to this goal, I thought that a checklist might be useful, giving the points to keep in mind when first assessing a situation and summarising features of effective crisis help.

I said at the beginning that it is only by facing and tolerating the pain of crisis that the hidden opportunity for personal development is revealed. I hope that this book will help you to help others face and tolerate that pain. When crisis is resolved well, the individual gains knowledge, renewed self-esteem and enhanced ability to cope with difficulties, both routine stress and future crisis. Seeing this happen, and knowing you have contributed to it, is very deeply rewarding.

BIBLIOGRAPHY

Breakwell, G. (1989) *Facing Physical Violence*. BPS Books/Routledge: Leicester.
Egan, G. (1985) *The Skilled Helper: Models, Skills and Methods for Effective Helping* (3rd edn). Brooks/Cole: Monterey Calif.
   A classic approach to counselling skills – clear and helpful.
Fontana, D. (1989) *Managing Stress*. BPS Books/Routledge: Leicester.
   A sister volume in this series; gives a very practical and useful approach to everyday stress. Many of the techniques would be useful following crisis.
Horowitz, M.J. (1986) *Stress Response Syndromes*. Jason Aronson: New York.
   A specialist book with some technical language – but don't be put off. It describes crisis response very clearly and is well worth the effort.
Pilisuk, M. & Parks, S.H. (1986) *The Healing Web. Social Networks and Human Survival*. University Press of New England: Hanover & London.
   Another specialist text but interesting and well written. Focuses on social networks and social support in human relationships and, indeed, in human survival.
Raphael, B. (1986) *When Disaster Strikes*. Hutchinson: London.
   A fine, readable book covering the issues involved in traumatic stress and disaster management.
Rowe, D. (1983) *Depression: The way out of your prison*. Routledge: London.
   A fascinating book written for the person suffering depression.
Worden, J.W. (1983) *Grief Counselling and Grief Therapy*. Tavistock: London.
   Very useful – describes specific methods of helping people who have been bereaved.

Box 7.1 Checklist: points to remember when first thinking about a crisis

- What is the stressful event that triggered the crisis?

- What are the stress features of the crisis event?
loss?	trauma?	disruption of routine?
negative revelation?	loss of control?	unexpectedness?
danger?	humiliation?	uncertain future?

- What is the core belief that the event challenges?

- If the crisis has been caused by the person's own actions, is there a possible hidden communication?

- What stages of crisis response has the individual experienced?
numbness?	anger?	depression?
avoidance?	shame?	active coping?
anxiety or panic?	guilt?	resolution?

- What kinds of coping has the individual been using?
  wishful thinking? suppression? distraction? self-talk?
  substance use (alcohol, drugs, food, etc)?
  emotional support from others?
  practical help from others?
  problem-solving? making plans?
  seeking information? lifestyle changes?

- What are the individual's sources of social support?
  social network – size
  social network – structure
  availability and mobilisation of: emotional support –
  companionship – information – practical help

- How can you promote a positive resolution?
  giving emotional support through good listening
  focusing on and clarifying the crisis response
  giving information
  liaising with others/networking the helpers
  teaching self-help skills (eg relaxation, self-talk)
  promoting the mobilisation of untapped social support

- How much can you realistically offer and for how long? This depends on:
  the nature of your professional role
  the individual's existing coping style
  the individual's social support
  your previous experience
  the level of distress you experience
  the availability of support to you as helper

ANSWERS TO EXERCISE 1

1. Almost always, but not always. Of course some crises cannot be avoided. It might be better to plan ahead so that the crisis is not necessary, but sometimes a crisis is necessary to make a hidden communication which would otherwise not be heeded.

2. We are often the unwitting and unwilling architects of our crises, but it is part of being human that crises can happen. Many crises are preventable – sometimes they result from not wanting to face up to something unpleasant. Others arise from circumstances very much out of our direct control, but we can still do a great deal to intensify or resolve the crisis.

3. No.

4. No, much longer for a major bereavement, if 'recover' is really the right word, since we are speaking of a life change, a transition. A two year period is a more realistic timescale for this.

5. Yes and no. There is a place for distracting oneself, but in order to bear the feelings not to make them go away. The feelings are very intense and it often helps to express them to a sympathetic listener.

6. Yes.

7. No, there is quite a lot they can do if they know *what* to do.

8. No. Post traumatic stress disorder entails much more than just having flashbacks which are a normal stress response.

9. Not necessarily.

10. Yes, true, probably due to preoccupation, poor concentration, tiredness and lack of physical co-ordination. Take extra care!

11. No, most severely stressful events are resolved within a natural social support system. Professional help is needed only if this is inadequate.

12. Not really, if getting back to normal means 'forget it and pull yourself together'. People need to maintain enough of their routine to provide a stable background, but allow space for the implications of the crisis to be worked through and that might mean things being 'abnormal' for quite a while. Again, the 'back to normal' approach implies that crisis is something to be got over with a return to the status quo; in fact it should lead to new insights and changed life in some respect.

13. No, it isn't just luck. A lot depends on the individual seeking the right help from the right people at the right time.

14. No, crisis is not just about emotions being out of control although powerful emotions are indeed part of the response to crisis.

ANSWERS TO EXERCISE 4

Compare your answers with these:
1. At least eight stressful events in this crisis:
    (a) Heavy loss at gambling.
    (b) First child born prematurely.

    (c)   Sudden death of mother.

    (d)   Creditor's letter theatening proceedings.

    (e)   Revelation to wife and family that he stole and lost money.

    (f)   Fight with brother-in-law.

    (g)   Separation from wife.

    (h)   Threat of dismissal from manager.

2.   (a)   Loss of money. No physical danger. Humiliation of misjudging the bet. Felt uncontrollable – had persuaded himself he could win his way out of trouble. Despite this the event is not entirely unexpected. No disruption of routine but increased uncertainty about the future.

    (b)   Loss of hope for a perfect, uncomplicated childbirth; danger of losing the child. Uncontrollable, unexpected but only minor humiliation. Routine disrupted by hospital visits. Future of child's health uncertain.

    (c)   Major loss of close tie – uncontrollable and unexpected bereavement. Loss of important hope of showing his mother her first grandchild. Disruption of routine – no longer regular visits to see her.

    (d)   Danger of prosecution. Threat of public humiliation. Threat of wife discovering his debts. Arises from his own actions and not entirely unexpected. Adds to uncertainty about the future.

    (e)   Threatened loss of his wife's respect. Major humiliation. Not entirely unexpected.

    (f)   Danger of physical injury. Anger might be warding off humiliation, guilt and shame. Not outside his own control, but fight itself not expected. Disrupted future routine and adds to uncertainty about the future.

    (g)   Major loss of close attachment. Had a general warning that this could happen due to previous events. Humiliation and severe disruption of daily routine.

    (h)   Humiliating confrontation. Threat of job loss unexpected as he thought he was buying time and getting away with faking results.

3.   Gambling loss → debts → creditor's letter → stealing money → family revelation & fight → separation → absenteeism & faking data → threat of dismissal.
Premature birth of child is independent stressor.
Death of mother is independent stressor.

4.   Core beliefs

    (i)   I am lucky – I can get something for nothing. I'm a winner.

    (ii)   My child is going to be healthy and strong. Illness and misfortune happen to other people, not me.

    (iii)   I will always have Mum there. I will have plenty of warning before I lose her. Death is controllable and distant.

    (iv)   I don't really have a gambling problem. Other people respect me.

    (v)   I am a valued member of my family.

    (vi)   My brother-in-law quite likes me and would help me out if I needed him to. I can control my temper.

    (vii) I am a good, lovable husband.

    (viii) I am a competent chemist. My firm values the work I have done and would overlook my problems.

5.   Many of his actions suggest avoidance – being unable to tolerate the feelings aroused by the earlier stressors. The humiliations involved in stress events (a), (d), (e), (g) and (h) may be causing feelings of shame or guilt. Anger is, possibly, a defensive reaction to ward off these feelings. The major losses in (c) and (g) are likely to lead to depression, empty feelings, sleep problems, loss of concentration and loss of interest in his work/leisure. Anxiety levels will be high in response to this level of threat and uncertainty. Denial, wishful thinking and alcohol use are his main coping strategies – emotion-focused strategies. Problem-focused coping is based on buying time and 'magical' solutions.

6.   The chemist has contributed a great deal to his own stress levels by these responses. Six of the eight events are caused by the avoidance responses described above. Only (c) and (d) are totally independent of his own actions.

ANSWERS TO EXERCISE 8

1.   *(a)*   Imposes the helper's frame of reference.
     (b)   Preferred response – reflects the woman's feelings.
     (c)   Helper is trying to avoid the feelings.

2.   *(a)*   Imposing helper's own view, not acknowledging the feelings.
     (b)   Preferred response; tries to speak to the underlying fear.
     (c)   Helper is avoiding the feeling, offering false reassurance.

3.   *(a)*   Preferred response – empathic but confronting the denial.
     (b)   Judgemental.
     (c)   Confrontational but not empathic.

4.   *(a)*   Unempathic and condescending.
     (b)   Judgemental.
     (c)   Preferred response; reflects the feelings and acknowledges loss.

5.   *(a)*   Not a bad response, but shies away from the feeling.
     (b)   Unhelpful – helper is frightened of the mother's feelings and is trying to avoid them.
     (c)   Preferred response, just 'staying with' how it feels.

6.   *(a)*   Unhelpful to ask questions.
     (b)   Helper is imposing his or her own feelings – the woman did not say she felt angry, but that she felt disgust and fear.
     (c)   Preferred response – empathic and caring.

ANSWERS TO EXERCISE 11

What could the chemist do to resolve the crisis?

Emotion-focused coping
Find whatever resources are necessary to be able to tolerate shame, depression and anxiety without constant avoidance, denial and palliative methods. In order to achieve this:

▶ Admit to himself he has a problem.

▶ Make a plan, set realistic goals

▶ Seek help – possibilities include:

  – someone to confide in and express feelings to about his losses
  – someone to give advice on debt management
  – skilled counselling re marital estrangement
  – self-help group e.g. *Gamblers Anonymous*
  – companionship, chance to get away from his problems

Self-care:
  – cut down drinking
  – eat properly
  – take exercise

Problem-focused coping
Tackle one problem at a time. Plan might include:

▶ Make a personal commitment to give up 'magical thinking'.

▶ Apologise to his estranged wife, to her sister and to his brother-in-law. Acknowledge to them that his behaviour was destructive and hurtful. Explain that he's trying to get himself sorted out, but don't ask them for help at this stage.

▶ Concentration loss, lack of energy etc. are to be expected following his bereavement and marital separation. With manager's help, find a way to tackle his job during this time without faking data or being absent. Negotiate a realistic agreement with employer about future behaviour.

▶ Work on reducing the anxiety and depression by self-care, confiding about losses and (if necessary) seeking professional help.

▶ Do not expect to solve all problems at once – stress responses make thinking straight difficult. Aim as a basic principle simply not to do anything that will make things worse than they are.

What could the manager do to help him?

▶ Offer a short-term counselling relationship focused on work-related problems but also allowing enough time to help him formulate a plan to tackle the debts, his gambling compulsion and his grief over his losses. Or, offer to find someone else (e.g. personnel manager) who can take this on but give your support and encouragement for him to attend these sessions.

▶ Explore with the chemist what other avenues of help are available to meet his other needs.

▶ Share with him your understanding of his crisis. Give praise and encouragement that he has finally had the courage to tell someone what is happening. Show compassion. Be sensitive to his feelings of humiliation and do not be judgemental.

▶ Be matter-of-fact about his work problem. Give clear messages about your expectations about absenteeism, drinking and faking data. Spell out what will happen if he does not comply but equally show him the positive route to regaining his self-esteem in his work.

▶ Reduce his workload temporarily. Acknowledge what he has been through and do not expect a normal standard of work performance whilst he is so depressed/anxious. On the other hand, don't treat him like a child or an 'invalid' – give him opportunities to achieve something worthwhile at work.

▶ If you feel you have useful knowledge and information to share, think carefully about how to time it. Is he ready to use it?

▶ Be consistent in following up your interest. Do be very firm about not tolerating self-destructive behaviour.

Acknowledgements

In writing this book I have drawn on the work of many psychologists, psychiatrists and social scientists. I am able to mention only a few of those who have influenced me in my approach to crisis: Chris Brewin, George Brown, Gerald Caplan, Mardi Horowitz, Stevan Hobfoll, Albert Kushlick, Richard Lazarus, Phil Mollon, Keith Oatley, Beverley Raphael, Dorothy Rowe, Anthony Ryle, John Teasdale, Peggy Thoits and Fraser Watts. To these and to many others I owe a great deal.

Note

The proper names and case illustrations in this book are fictitious, although drawn as composites from many similar situations which I have observed during my clinical and research practice. None of the examples represents any one individual and any resemblance to particular individuals is coincidental.

INDEX